THE ULTIMATE INTERCULTURAL QUESTION BOOK

The Ultimate Intercultural Question Book

1000+ QUESTIONS TO DEEPEN YOUR INTERCULTURAL INTERACTIONS

Marco Blankenburgh

CONTENTS

PREFACE

Why a book of questions?

Being knowledgeable has always been important to me, but after relocating six times, it became apparent that being a skilled learner is far more important than simply knowing, or rather, assuming to know.

I first moved to another country and culture in 1985, when I was eighteen. Little did I know that moving around the world would become a significant part of my life. I subsequently moved again in 1988, 1989, 1992, and 1999. Finally, as a twenty-three-year-old arriving in the Middle Eastern context, I began to realize that learning about individuals and their cultures was far more valuable than merely possessing knowledge about general cultures or relying on my presumed answers. I saw that I could not rely on external characteristics such as skin color, mannerisms, accent, or even the passport people carry. So, I shifted my focus to learning about culture and people directly from the individuals themselves.

As I grew in the realization that each person carries their own uniquely wired cultural identity despite the broad cultural or language groupings into which they fall, it became increasingly apparent that questions were the key to unlocking a true understanding of everyone I encountered. This was a wakeup call for me because I love knowledge, ideas, and research. Thus, I had to replace my static research of culture with a dynamic, agile desire to learn individual cultures.

Every good student knows that good learning comes from good questions. When working with people, knowing how to ask questions is the gateway to gaining true insight into individuals and engaging in effective, relationship-building conversations. Asking good questions, in particular, allows us to delve beyond the surface and gain a genuine understanding of people and culture.

This realization sparked the intercultural work on which KnowledgeWorkx is based. One of the things we're passionate about here at KnowledgeWorkx is being cultural learners. To be a cultural learner, one must assume that they don't know—that they don't have all the answers. They rely on questions to learn of others' cultures. That is why it was an exciting development when one of the practitioners using KnowledgeWorkx' cultural framework, Spencer MacCuish, provided us with an initial list of just over 100 cultural acquisition questions. This list served as a great starting point.

As we used and shared the questions on the list, we discovered the power of good questions in equipping people to engage in deep conversations and truly delve into the richness of who individuals really are.

Exploring the richness of personal cultural stories and journeys, we saw that the deep respect these questions paid to others had a powerful impact on relationships. We even heard about how this initial list of questions helped long-standing friends learn things about each other that they had never known before. Another person felt they had learned more about their friend in an hour than in the past five years of friendship due to the intentional questions.

This was an exciting development for us as it showed that there was a need for an increased focus on asking questions to create room to hear someone's story more wholly. Asking those questions invites others to tell their story alongside ours, which then creates space for a new shared cultural space.

These questions have resulted in deeper understanding and insight into the differences (but more so similarities) between people. They create room for stories, and now, more than ever in this modern world, we need to allow people to tell their stories. It is significant to have a powerful tool such as this one, which facilitates telling your own story and listening to the stories of others.

Some of the beauty of sharing our individual stories may lie in finding the spaces and places where we have walked the same road and using those to tell about a joint journey. We could use these common spaces and places to create our own unique culture where the space is as much mine as it is yours, where my culture does not come at the expense of yours.

How You Can Use This Book

With this book, you will have a framework that leads to more meaningful conversations, especially when it comes to crossing cultural boundaries. Not just for conversations between a person from one country relating to someone from another, we're talking about intercultural conversations between two people who are uniquely wired, cultural, human beings. Through these questions, you can listen without presumption to the journeys and experiences that have shaped others despite where they are from and what we expect them to say. We hope you will use this book to build relational bridges and allow space for people to tell their story. That is why this book is close to my heart, and I hope through your conversations it becomes close to yours too.

This is only the beginning. We hope that this will be the first of several versions of this book. As we discover more questions, we will create more open spaces where more people can tell more stories and be allowed to connect to each other in deeper ways. And invariably, ask more questions. We hope that this cycle will continue and go from strength to strength in equipping people around the world with tools to connect more effectively, and more meaningfully with one another.

THE KNOWLEDGEWORKX FRAMEWORK: INTERCULTURAL AGILITY

"a nationality and ethnicity-oriented approach of looking at culture was insufficient to engage people effectively in a multicultural world"

"Every person is on their own unique cultural journey and as a result has developed their own unique cultural wiring."

a. Intercultural Agility

Out of that great realization, KnowledgeWorkx was born and with it came a new framework addressing one of the greatest challenges of our globalized world: meaningful human relationship and connection.

The way in which KnowledgeWorkx empowers individuals to navigate relating in a global world is through what we call Intercultural Agility. We take a dynamic approach, equipping you to read culturally diverse situations in real-time, so that you can anticipate, correctly interpret, adjust, and respond tactfully in any context.

The Intercultural Agility framework weaves history, research, and real-world experience into a tool which unlocks deep cultural understanding. This chapter will dive into the different facets of Intercultural Agility, starting with the way we view culture.

"Intercultural Agility is not simply having the knowledge of both the visible and invisible aspects of culture. It also requires the skill of analysis -- knowing how to most effectively deepen that knowledge. This, in turn, allows us to move towards a deeper understanding of the culture as it is experienced by the insiders. Developing Intercultural Agility is key for effectiveness in a cross-cultural setting, no matter the type of work."

—Joann Pitmann

b. Self-Cultural Analysis

The world has become more globalized than ever before. In 2020, over 281 million people lived in a different country from their passport[1]. A third of the global workforce is engaged

---

[1](n.d.). World Migration Report 2022. World Migration Report. Retrieved March 19, 2024, from https://worldmigrationreport.iom.int/wmr-2022-interactive/

across diversities and across borders every day. While that number is large and can feel like just a statistic, it's likely that you can think of someone right now who fits into that category. Maybe even *you* do! There has been a significant rise in working virtually, which has resulted in being able to hire talent, serve customers, and offer support from anywhere to anywhere.

Research shows that, due to humanity's interconnectedness, will need to become "more human humans": better at listening, better at asking questions, collaborating, innovating, communicating, developing ourselves, managing people, negotiating, and navigating complex problems together.

Diverse and intercultural teams are becoming the norm, and we need to up our game in order to be "more human humans" across cultures. In this new reality, we have a significant challenge that needs to be addressed: we still insist on explaining who we are as cultural human beings through the lenses of nationality and ethnicity. Unfortunately, boxing people in based on those classifications is often done outside the context of relationships. As a result, it doesn't lead to meaningful connection, and even causes people to drift apart.

It is our mission to change this. We need a new way of looking at who we are as cultural beings. We are not saying that nationality, ethnicity, and race are not important, but we are saying that they are inadequate starting points for developing meaningful and productive relationships. Consider the story of my colleague Ashni; while she may be Indian by nationality, she is someone very different when it comes to the way she identifies herself as a cultural human being. Her Hindi is not that great, and she has lived most of her life in another country. Ashni considers herself an NRI or non-resident Indian but is mistaken for a local when in India because that is who she is on the outside. You would never know who Ashni really is by assuming her language or culture based on the shell of nationality.

So, we have developed a multi-faceted approach that allows you to get to know every person as an individual with their own unique cultural wiring whose depth and richness is uncovered through learning, or how we like to put it, question-asking.

c. Issues that led us to find a new approach

The world has become more global than ever before. Even if you have not made efforts to reach out to the world, the world has come to you. We engage the world through the Internet, games, sports, the entertainment industry, news, education, work, and even the people who live next door.

In this global and diverse world, we still sit on a strange notion: the insistence that culture has to be understood through the lenses of nationality and ethnicity. In 2004, we realized this was not going to work for the globalized world we live in today. Although your new colleague may carry a Swedish passport, how do you know if they match the "blueprint" of a "true Swede"? What if you pull out your "cheat sheet for working with Swedes" only to discover that your new Swedish colleague is a global nomad who was born in Sudan and has lived on four continents before finishing high school? (This is actually one of my colleagues)

d. The radical new idea

After plowing through a whole bunch of books that used nationality and ethnicity as a way to guide the reader in intercultural relationships, we realized that trying to live and become more effective in relationships with this nationality-driven grid was a challenge. Not only was it impossible to memorize over 200 cheat sheets for every possible nationality, but it was also dangerous in a world where hundreds of millions of people are "cultural composites" of the rich cultural journeys that they and the generations before them have been on in life.

The more we looked at this, the more we realized that a nationality and ethnicity-oriented approach of looking at culture was insufficient to engage people effectively in a multicultural world.

Within the field of psychology, many psychometric instruments have been developed to help people understand themselves and relate to others. Experts have attempted to "map out" the terrain of human personality from various angles. In talking to psychologists, there is a common assumption that the world of psychology can explain most of what is going on in human behavior but living and interacting with many different cultures in Dubai in the early 2000s, we found that to be profoundly incomplete.

Our experience underlined a problem: that by emphasizing the psychological side of behavior so much, the cultural side of behavior has been underemphasized.

Looking at the number of assessments available on each side of the equation, there are hundreds of tools on the psychology of human behavior, but as of the publishing of this book, we had found only fifty-four assessments on the cultural side of the equation[2] (https://inter-culturalintelligence.com).

So, we asked the question: "Why can't we map out personal cultural preferences like we do personality ones?"

We started pursuing that goal in 2002, coining the term "Self-Cultural Analysis", committing to never use these tools to create averages or stereotypes for countries.

---

[2] KnowledgeWorkx (n.d.). Online Intercultural Tools. Inter-Culturalintelligence.com. Retrieved August 26, 2024, from https://inter-culturalintelligence.com/intercultural_tools/

e. What is Self-Cultural Analysis

We set out to develop a framework that creates a structure and language for specifically the culturally driven behavior of humans around the world.

We were not the first to try and create a framework that explains human cultural behavior. Many researchers have worked with dimensions, polarities, or values that seem to manifest themselves more strongly in various cultures. We stand on the shoulders of these researchers and are very grateful for the work they have done, but we wanted to make these frameworks more practical.

We looked specifically at the work of people like E.T. Hall, G. Hofstede, and F.J. Trompenaars and asked the question: "When I meet somebody for the first time, what would I want to know about that person to understand who they are as a cultural being? What is truly relevant and meaningful to assist me in building a strong relationship with them?"

Using their research, we have created a framework for Self-Cultural Analysis that allows us to *measure personal cultural behavioral preferences – not just trends in larger populations.* We do that for ourselves first and then as a grid for understanding others.

We have developed two Self-Cultural Analysis tools: The Three Colors of Worldview© and the Cultural Mapping Inventory© based on the 12 Dimensions of Culture©.

f. How does Self-Cultural Analysis work

Self-Cultural Analysis starts with understanding the cultural motivators and demotivators we bring into any relationship; drivers that run deeper than actual behaviors. We call these the Three Colors of Worldview©.

The Three Colors of Worldview© map out three main cultural drivers:

- Doing the right thing and avoiding the wrong thing - Innocence/Guilt
- Doing what is honorable and avoiding what is shameful - Honor/Shame
- Doing what gives you power and avoiding situations where your power is diminished - Power/Fear

Knowing the cultural drivers that we bring into a conversation is the key to getting started. Cultural drivers impact the way we develop trust, handle conflict, lead a team, and engage effectively with clients. We have developed an online cultural assessment to help you understand your mix of these cultural drivers and how they affect your behavioral choices.

On its own, The Three Colors of Worldview© is merely a starting point. It doesn't give the language and analysis framework necessary to understand any possible intercultural situation.

Seventeen years ago, we researched every cultural dimension we found documented in academia and asked ourselves the question: "If we were to develop an assessment tool with the framework and language to make sense of any intercultural situation; which dimensions would it need to include?"

From this, we developed the Cultural Mapping Inventory©, built on twelve cultural dimensions. This inventory is designed to accompany the Three Colors of Worldview© and creates a comprehensive Self-Cultural Analysis framework. We have proven time and again that these tools work harmoniously to create a robust framework for analyzing any intercultural situation.

The twelve dimensions of the Cultural Mapping Inventory© form an excellent foundation to discuss personal cultural preferences, explaining the "why" of intercultural dilemmas and the behaviors of individuals and groups involved in them. They give us a neutral language to discuss the intercultural dynamics at play, leveling the playing field and balancing out those inclined to be critical of cultures different from their own.

g. How does Self-Cultural Analysis change the game?

If our mind is programmed to look for cultural clues based on a person's nationality or ethnicity, we are likely to get stuck on stereotypes and miss a great deal of what is important about others. But by starting our journey of cultural discovery with the premise that each person has their own unique cultural preferences, we are defining a fundamentally different way of engaging with the person in front of us. Nationality and ethnicity become just one factor in a person's cultural makeup.

Self-Cultural Analysis gives us a new level of respect for individuals; the type of respect that communicates to the other party: "You are a unique person, and I want to get to know who you are. I believe that your personal cultural preferences are important for us to build a meaningful relationship." Starting with the philosophy of Self-Cultural Analysis allows us to ask different questions; ones that lead to richer, deeper, and more respectful conversations and relationships.

Self-Cultural Analysis has proven to be a pragmatic game changer. In sales and customer service, if I have a deeper understanding of clients' unique cultural wiring, I am enabled to come alongside them constructively, resulting in productive relationships and greater client satisfaction. In leadership, if I become more sensitive to the unique cultural wiring of the people I lead, I can build stronger teams by tailoring my leadership approach and crafting a team culture that resonates with everyone.

As every person is on their own unique cultural journey and as a result has developed their own unique cultural wiring, we have developed the Self-Cultural Analysis approach. Seeing every person as a uniquely wired human being is a powerful and liberating starting point for developing your Intercultural Agility.

You can read more about the KnowledgeWorkx Framework at: www.knowledgeworkx.com/framework

TEAM

What makes a team successful?

When a group of individuals collaborates toward a shared objective, their collective impact can exceed the sum of their individual efforts. However, effective teamwork requires more than just shared goals; it demands cohesion, trust, and open communication.

It would be wonderful if everything was always "awesome" and "cool when you're part of a team[3]", but teams, like other aspects of life, cannot always be as jovial and pleasant as we would like them to be.

In recent years, the dynamics of teamwork have evolved, particularly with the rise of remote work. While synergy can be challenging to achieve even in traditional settings, the distance imposed by remote work can further hinder the development

---

[3] *Lego Movie. (2014). [Film]. Hollywood: Warner Animation, Village Roadshow Pictures, Lego System A/S, Vertigo Entertainment.*

of genuine connections and mutual trust among team members.

While working on a remote team like that, Helen saw consistent evidence of the team breaking down, which snowballed into significant miscommunications; colleagues regarded each other with suspicion, which led to further conflicts of different kinds. All this contributed to a growing resentment on the team. Upon reflection as an Intercultural Agility practitioner, Helen identified four crucial components that were absent and impeding the team's progress:

- **Behavior-based Trust**

Establishing an environment where team members have confidence that their colleagues will follow through on commitments.

- **Aligning Purpose**

Ensuring clarity of purpose and providing opportunities to celebrate successes and address setbacks together.

- **Overcoming Communication Challenges**

Fostering active listening and empathy to mitigate misunderstandings that often lead to conflict and resentment.

- **Developing Relational Capital**

Creating space for personal stories and experiences to foster deeper connections and break down interpersonal barriers.

Recognizing the detrimental impact of these deficiencies on team dynamics, Helen took proactive steps to address the underlying issues. By prioritizing dedicated time for the team to engage in active listening and story-sharing, Helen facilitated the development of relational capital and trust. As tensions eased and communication improved, individual team members transitioned into collaborative partners united in pursuit of a common goal.

Getting the Conversation Started
Characteristics of a Team

1. What is meant by "teaming," and how does it differ from traditional teamwork?
2. In your culture, is the concept of "teaming" highly regarded? What factors contribute to its value or lack thereof?
3. What is the primary purpose of assembling a team in your perspective?
4. What three essential qualities do you believe are necessary for a strong and successful team, and why are these qualities significant?
5. How do you instill the value of teamwork and being a team player in children?
6. In your opinion, how crucial is teamwork in achieving goals and fostering success in various aspects of life?

Roles on a Team

7. What specific role do you like playing on teams, and why?
8. Where did you first learn how to be a team-player?
9. Reflecting on your experiences, how easy or difficult is it for you to work on a team?
10. In your opinion, what characteristics and behaviors define a "good team leader"?
11. What qualities do you believe constitute an effective team player, and why are these qualities important?
12. Can you share an example of the best team you've been a part of, and what made it exceptional in your view?

Teams at Work

13. When, if ever, is it appropriate to have side-conversations during a team meeting, and why?
14. Can you describe a negative experience from the worst team you've been a part of, and what factors contributed to its dysfunctionality?
15. What is the role of social time in a team and how does it impact overall team performance?
16. What are reasonable expectations regarding "outside of work" social activities for team members?
17. If you were leading a team, what types of social activities would you organize to foster camaraderie and team cohesion?
18. How would you address underperformance by a team member within the group?
19. What factors contribute to creating a productive environment for teams, and conversely, what elements can make an environment unproductive for teamwork?

"IA becomes a kind of computer board or operating system that, by getting rightly established, allows us to engage all the other actionable needs of the group, the family, the team, the company, etc."

—Jim Foster

People are multifaceted individuals with diverse social, emotional, psychological, intellectual, and cultural backgrounds, each on their unique journey. While common interests often form connections that evolve into relationships, a deeper connection may be necessary for individuals to effectively collaborate toward a shared goal. Whether the goal is professional, athletic, religious, or social, a team composed of diverse individuals may encounter challenges in working together with purpose and synergy.

These diverse cultural journeys contribute to the dynamics and interactions within a team. Acknowledging and respecting each person's unique journey can foster a culture of trust and belonging, facilitating the team's ability to achieve its objectives.

During an international team gathering in his hometown of Puerto Rico, Javier experienced tension between two groups within the team: members from Canada and the United States who had traveled to join the gathering, and local Puerto Ricans attending the event.

Javier noticed his own discomfort with the strictly business-oriented conversations of his international teammates, who seemed focused solely on task-related matters without allowing the discussion to drift into personal topics. From their perspective, the North American team members felt that they needed to move the proceedings along without wasting any time. In contrast, the Puerto Rican colleagues felt frustrated by the lack of opportunity to connect on a more personal level and were willing to extend meeting times to hear each other's stories and foster inclusivity.

While the team's communication styles and attitudes toward time management differed, neither group was inherently wrong. These differences represent just a few dimensions of cultural variation among team members. Interculturally agile individuals like Javier can play a crucial role in facilitating understanding and finding common ground within the team. By sharing insights about cultural differences and providing language to navigate them, Javier and others can help the team embrace diversity and thrive collectively.

Digging Deeper

Team Dynamics

20. When you're a member of a team, do you typically address conflicts directly or indirectly? What factors influence your approach?
21. Why do you think teamwork can be challenging in certain environments or situations?
22. What do you find fulfilling or joyful about being part of a team?
23. What are some common challenges or difficulties experienced when working in a team?
24. In your experience, how is exceptional work recognized within a team?
25. In your opinion, how should a healthy team approach and manage conflicts?
26. In team meetings, how would disagreement typically be handled?
27. Do you believe that cultural diversity is important for team performance? Why or why not?
28. How does your team encourage and embrace ethnic diversity among its members?

Loyalty and Trust

29. What things are essential for building trust in a team?
30. How do you show loyalty to your team and how far would you go to express that loyalty?
31. How do you handle team members who exhibit toxic behavior?
32. Who is responsible for a team's success, and why do you hold this view?

"So many common team functions- expectations and norms in communication, conflict resolution, good teamwork, leadership, etc., are shaped by our respective cultures. Learning about what is beneath the surface of our behaviors and actions, going beyond the stereotype single story we might first see, can help us grow in understanding, collaboration, and effectiveness as we serve and collaborate."

—Samantha Deck

TIME

How should time be spent?

It flies when you're having fun, it crawls when you're not. . . time is always passing, and whether we're aware of it or not, every person, as part of their unique cultural makeup, has a specific orientation to it.

Axel, a German team lead, was assigned a project and had a video call scheduled with Rohaan, a potential partner from Pakistan. They had exchanged only brief emails prior to the call and didn't know much about each other. Axel, who would describe himself as direct, effective, and time-focused, joined the call prepared to discuss the project and make decisions promptly. He was rigid in sticking to the allotted time for the meeting, interrupting the conversation several times to make sure they stayed on track. The call ended on time, and both men returned to their day.

In hindsight, Axel realized that he and Rohaan had different expectations for the call. While Axel prioritized discussing the project efficiently, Rohaan was trying to connect with Axel and enjoy interaction beyond business matters.

The contrasting views on time between Axel and Rohaan were not inherently right or wrong but simply different. Axel's reflection on this highlighted the importance of considering these differences in future interactions with Rohaan, perhaps by initiating discussions to better understand their differing perspectives.

Getting the Conversation Started
General

1. Is time considered abundant or valuable in your culture? Why is it regarded in this way?

2. Is it good to be in a hurry?
3. What are culturally acceptable reasons for being late?
4. Why do certain cultures place a strong emphasis on punctuality?
5. How is time typically allocated and utilized in your society?

Professional life

6. Would arriving late to a meeting or event be considered impolite in your culture?
7. What are the durations of typical work meetings? Additionally, what proportion of these meetings is dedicated to building relationships, and what proportion is focused on accomplishing tasks?
8. In your culture, is it acceptable to close the doors to meetings once they have begun to prevent latecomers from entering?
9. If someone arrives late to an in-person meeting while you have arrived on time, how do you usually handle the situation?

10. How far in advance do you typically schedule meetings in your culture?
11. Are there specific types of meetings where flexibility or tardiness is acceptable, while punctuality is crucial for others?

Friends

12. Do you typically schedule time to meet with family or close friends, or do these meetings happen more spontaneously in your culture?
13. In your culture, how would someone be perceived if they abruptly ended a lengthy conversation in order to be on time for their next appointment?
14. Would you be offended if someone came an hour late to a dinner invitation?
15. If a close friend drops by unexpectedly but you have an important meeting to attend, how would you typically handle that situation?
16. In your culture, would it be acceptable to arrive late when meeting an important person, or is punctuality expected regardless of the circumstances?

Ron and Lydia have encountered challenges with timing, even among people from the same culture. While individuals often adhere to what is considered "normal" for their cultural background, everyone expresses this aspect of their personality in unique ways.

The couple participates in a Thai Bible study group, and they often offer a ride to a Thai woman, Kamlai, who lives in their apartment complex. Although the Bible study has a set start time, it is not strictly enforced, but most attendees make an effort to arrive on time.

However, Ron and Lydia frequently find themselves arriving

almost thirty minutes late because of the time it takes for Kamlai to be ready. This situation puts them in a difficult position, and it is inconvenient for the rest of the group. However, they are hesitant to confront Kamlai and potentially embarrass her.

A culturally sensitive way to address the issue could be for Ron and Lydia to initiate a general conversation about punctuality with Kamlai. They could then share their own perspectives on the importance of being on time, providing a context for discussing their need to adhere to schedules without directly criticizing her tardiness. This approach allows them to address the issue respectfully and maintain Kamlai's dignity.

Digging Deeper
Personal

17. Do you feel like you control your time or does time control you?
18. Is punctuality an important concept in your community?
19. How do you organize and manage your time?
20. In general, do you feel you have enough time?
21. What are typical sayings that relate to time in your culture?
22. What is your view of time and how do you show you value the time you have been given?
23. How do you wish you prioritized your time?
24. What do your weekends look like, are they booked full or free-flowing; what do you typically spend your weekend time on?

Search for Meaning

25. What is more important, showing people you care by being on time for them or showing them you care by being willing to be late for them?
26. Do you move into the future, or does the future come to you? Why do you believe that?
27. Is it possible to make up for lost time? How would you do that?
28. Is there a connection between how people handle time and their reliability and trustworthiness?
29. What is considered an appropriate way for older people to use their time?
30. Is your life worth living? What makes it worthwhile?

TRUST

What Makes You Worthy of Trust?

Trust, once broken, is difficult to earn again. It is a foundational element in human relationships, crucial for building communities and fostering connections among individuals. When you trust someone, you confide in them, come to them for advice, seek their help in times of need, and even welcome them into your family. Conversely, when you don't trust someone, you are likely to keep your distance or choose not to have any contact with them at all.

Cultural perspectives often shape how trust is perceived and established. In some cultures, trust is freely given and expected from the outset, even in professional settings. However, in other cultures, trust must be earned through consistent behavior over time. When individuals from different cultural backgrounds interact, discrepancies in understanding and expectations regarding trust can arise, potentially straining relationships.

Zephen's experience highlights the clash of cultural norms

surrounding trust in a business context. As a representative agent with a solid reputation, Zephen was accustomed to being trusted by his business partners. It came as a shock and even an offense when he was asked to sign a confidentiality agreement by a German-based corporation he had worked with for some time. To him, the confidentiality agreement implied a lack of trust and undermined the years of rapport he had built with the company. The company, on the other hand, viewed the agreement as a standard procedure designed to protect sensitive information, not indicative of any distrust toward their partners. Recognizing the cultural differences at play, the representative from the company took the time to explain the rationale behind the agreement and reassure Zephen of the company's continued trust and respect for their partnership.

Through open dialogue and cultural understanding, both parties were able to overcome their initial misinterpretations and reaffirm their mutual trust and respect. The experience served as a learning opportunity, allowing them to deepen their understanding of each other's cultural norms and communication styles. Ultimately, their relationship emerged stronger from the encounter, demonstrating the power of effective communication and cultural sensitivity in building and maintaining trust.

Getting the Conversation Started
Establishing trust

1. What does it mean to trust another person?
2. What behaviors can either build or destroy trust?
3. What qualities make a person trustworthy?
4. How can trust be developed at personal, interpersonal, and community levels?

5. Can you give examples of how products are more or less trusted based on where they were produced, or which company produced them?
6. Which leadership roles in society are generally perceived as trustworthy or untrustworthy, and have these perceptions changed over the past few generations?
7. What are some common tactics criminals use to exploit trust and deceive people out of money or possessions?

Maintaining trust

8. How can individuals show that they are trustworthy?
9. Can you recall a time when someone betrayed your trust? If so, how did it happen?

Restoring trust

10. What does it take to restore trust after it has been broken?
11. Are there cultural rituals that help in restoring trust when it is broken?
12. Have you ever broken someone's trust? Describe what you did to regain it.
13. What did you have to do to restore the relationship when you broke someone's trust?
14. To what extent does one's outward appearance influence the level of trust they receive from others?
15. When someone is forgiven, does this automatically imply that they have also regained the person's trust? Why or why not?

At times, a person gives their trust by proxy, or on blind faith. This is an essential part of the business world and is central to the success of networking. When someone you trust recommends you get to know or hire someone they trust, you take their word for it.

Ray, a franchisor from New York, found himself engaged in a complex multi-million-dollar deal with a Chinese Area Developer who was developing stores in China for Ray's company. There was much to be lost on both sides and trust was essential to the success of the operations. Everything got off to a quick and smooth start. Each man was passionate about the project and ready to see it succeed, putting in the work where needed. However, with time, distrust began to seep into their relationship. Ray was not familiar with the concept of "saving face", a common practice in Chinese culture. On some occasions, the Area Director would choose his words carefully or leave out details in order to prevent shame, but this left Ray feeling misled and undermined. His trust was eroding and a solution was needed for the project to continue.

Ray decided to leverage his existing relationship with the Vice President of Operations in the Chinese company, an individual he trusted and respected. The VP of Operations was brought into meetings and delegations, which put Ray at ease and allowed for the two companies to find a way to continue the development project with all parties confident in its success.

This story underscores the critical role of trust in business relationships, especially when navigating cultural differences. It highlights the importance of understanding cultural nuances

and leveraging trusted connections to overcome challenges and ensure the success of collaborative ventures.

Digging Deeper

16. To what extent do you value trust in relationships with people who are close to you?
17. To what extent does keeping your word equate to being trustworthy?

18. How do you build trust with your spouse or partner?
19. How many people do you genuinely trust in your life?
20. When it comes to legally binding decisions, would you take someone at their word or require a contract? Why?
21. How do you build trust in your culture?
22. Do you believe it is acceptable to break a promise? If not, why?
23. How much do ethnic or religious backgrounds influence trust or distrust between groups in society?
24. Were there specific nationalities or ethnicities you were taught to trust or distrust growing up, and what were the reasons given for those beliefs?

Leadership/authority (in public and private life)

25. Are leaders in various societal roles expected to maintain consistency in their public and private lives in order to gain your trust?
26. What are the potential consequences of placing trust in someone?
27. Do you tend to trust authority figures or approach them with skepticism? Why do you feel that way?
28. How does your society treat people who are in authority (politicians, law enforcement. . .) once they have proven themself untrustworthy? Are they able to maintain their position?
29. Can you recall recent instances in your community where trust was broken or restored, indicating a trend of either growing or declining trust?
30. Do you or have you ever entrusted important decisions in your life, such as marriage, family, or career choices, to someone else?
31. In your community, can you think of recent stories of broken or restored trust that seem to indicate a growth or erosion of trust?

WORK RELATIONSHIPS

What does friendship at work look like?

Do you enjoy working with your coworkers? The average person spends almost a third of their life at work4, so working professionals could spend more time throughout the week with their coworkers than their own families. Whether you spend forty hours a week in the office or only interact virtually, work relationships are complicated and often the determining factor in whether a person looks forward to or dreads going to the office.

Everyone has different ways of connecting. Some individuals easily connect with others, while some prefer more formal interactions. It's essential to recognize that these preferences are varied and not necessarily tied to nationality or culture.

Monica's experience highlights the impact of differing

---

4 In: 41. One third of your life is spent at work. Gettysburg.edu. Retrieved December 6, 2023, from https://gettysburg.edu/news/stories?id=7d87b34-650c-4f48-9e32-4b09ea48e72b

communication styles and approaches to building relationships in the workplace. She approached work relationships informally, enjoying small talk before getting to her tasks. She felt that knowing her coworkers made work more enjoyable, allowing for smoother collaboration and better listening. She often worked with Juan Pablo, who didn't chat much, and when there was something that needed to get done, he would let Monica know the task and move on. Monica, being so personable, felt incredibly disrespected when he repeatedly did this instead of engaging in conversation with her in friendly way.

Despite being skilled professionals, Monica and Juan Pablo's inability to understand each other's personal culture and communication preferences resulted in conflict, ultimately leading to Monica's resignation. Had they discussed their approaches to communication and relationship-building, they may have resolved their differences more effectively.

Getting the Conversation Started
Coworkers

1. What does friendship look like in an office environment? Are there specific behaviors or interactions that define workplace friendships?
2. To what extent do you believe it's important to invest in work relationships? Why?
3. During lunch or coffee breaks, do colleagues tend to eat together or alone? What factors influence this behavior?
4. Are your relationships at work strictly business-related, or do you interact with your colleagues in a personal capacity? Why do you prefer your relationships that way?
5. What characteristics define a good work relationship? Is it primarily about productivity, friendliness, strategic importance, collaboration potential, or a combination of these factors?

6. Do you enjoy attending work parties? Can you explain the reasons behind your preference?
7. If you're close with your colleagues, do you socialize with them outside of work? What types of activities do you typically engage in together?
8. To what extent do you share personal matters with your coworkers? Are you aware of details about your coworkers' families, hobbies, or other personal aspects of their lives?
9. What does it take for your work friendships to become personal friendships?
10. Do you consider your work friends to be as close as your "real friends" outside of work, or do you perceive a distinction between the two? Why or why not?

Hiring

11. What are the most prevalent methods for securing employment through friendship connections in your experience or observation?
12. What are the potential benefits and drawbacks of giving friends and family preferential treatment during the recruitment process?
13. To what extent can employees be considered "untouchable" within an organization because of their friendship connections?

Social events

14. Is it acceptable to organize "fun" events such as celebrations and holiday parties in the workplace? What are the potential benefits or drawbacks of such activities?
15. How would you react if a coworker contacted your family without your consent to arrange a celebration or event for you?

Performance/Team Dynamics

16. If somebody is underperforming on a team, to what extent is this change how the matter addressed if a friendship has formed between the superior and the subordinate?
17. How are disagreements handled on your team once friendships have formed between team members?

"As our company expands globally into new countries and regions, the range of cultural differences amongst our employee population grows exponentially. Understanding what influences our worldview, communication style, and what might get in the way of healthy and objective collaboration is critical for our internal company relations. Learning more about ourselves, as well as those that may see the world very differently from us will proactively help to reduce friction, future conflict or complications, and enable smooth coexistence and productivity."—Miguel Poblete

---

Roman was put in a unique situation involving work relationships that required him to use deftness and cultural intelligence. A charity he was involved with in Belgium went through a change of leadership. The previous manager was close friends with a Sri Lankan man named Stephen who did a lot for the organization. The new manager was not comfortable with the informal, and seemingly less professional, way that Stephen dealt with various tasks (employing people "off the books" to save money, relying on relationships rather than contracts, asking for small favors frequently). Roman was asked to help communicate the need for a more formal arrangement with Stephen.

Stephen and Roman had a good working and personal relationship—which was instrumental in maintaining accord on all sides. Stephen had no problem being frank with him about his dislike of the new leadership and assumed Roman was on his side. This helped keep the situation less adversarial but also made it difficult to communicate the need for more boundaries and formality. Roman tried to engage Stephen on a relational level, explaining to him the difference in approach between the previous manager and the new one, highlighting the fact that both had their strengths; from there, he tried to explain that ultimately it was not only for the charity's but also for Stephen's protection that they begin utilizing more strict regulations.

Stephen was very gracious about it all, and never wanted to see Roman as anything but on his side. He understood that the requests for more formality required Roman to change the way he was doing things as well. It touched Roman that Stephen would never even entertain the idea that he was in any way not on his team.

This scenario is an example of the power of a strong work relationship. Had the wrong person approached Stephen about his manner of working, he could have been greatly hurt and offended. Roman knew his role in Stephen's work and personal life and was able to save face on many sides.

Digging Deeper
Hierarchy

18. If you need a favor from a coworker in a different department, are you able to ask for this favor directly, or do you have to ask his or her boss?
19. Are you more comfortable in a highly structured environment where it is clear who is the leader and who is the follower?
20. How are meetings expected to run in your culture? Who leads them, and who is only required to participate?
21. What would happen if you challenged your superior in front of other staff members?
22. In what circumstances is it appropriate to voice a concern or question to your superior and does this change if they are your friend?
23. How friendly and approachable should a leader be to their team?
24. How are the principles you use to lead at work different or similar to the ones you use in your family?

Client Relationships

25. Is the customer always right or are there instances when they are not?
26. How do you relate to or connect with customers?
27. Where will you draw the line between giving a client an excellent experience and maintaining dignity and respect of your team?
28. Should loyalty be viewed as the highest priority in a relationship with a supplier, or should another value be prioritized? Why do you say so?

29. Are the personal relationships you build with clients and suppliers for the purpose of work, or are they real friends?
30. To what extent is it appropriate to give special favors or discounts to clients who are family members or friends?

Bosses

31. Who decides what the expectations are in a relationship outside the office—your boss or you?
32. Is it acceptable to be friends with your boss?
33. Are romantic relationships with co-workers or bosses permissible and are there rules about how they should be conducted?
34. How would you respond if your boss invited you to watch a movie with them, or do something social outside of work hours?

LEADERSHIP AND FOLLOWERSHIP

Who should we follow and why?

"Leadership is influence - nothing more, nothing less."[5] These striking words by John C. Maxwell challenge us to recognize the places where we have influence; places where we are leading without realizing it.

Regardless of the type of group—sports team, organization, company, community project, or political party—it can be assumed that there will be a person, or group of people, who go ahead of the group while others follow in response to guidance and direction. These relationships between leaders and followers should not be taken lightly. So, how you lead will determine whether those behind you will follow.

5 Maxwell, John C. (2005) The 360 degree leader: developing your influence from anywhere in the organization. California: Nelson Business

Consider Dennis, who led a non-profit organization with a loyal administrator, Paulo, managing office affairs. In an attempt to lighten Paulo's workload, Dennis hired an assistant reporting directly to him (Dennis). However, this decision unintentionally created tension in the office. Dennis was unaware of the underlying issues until he realized Paulo felt slighted and undermined by the assistant's presence. In response, Paulo began undermining the assistant, leading to a tense working environment.

Had Dennis understood Paulo's Power/Fear worldview, he might have seen that hiring the assistant altered the hierarchy for Paulo, causing him to feel betrayed. With this insight, Dennis could have navigated the transition more effectively by validating Paulo's importance and reassuring him of his value in the organization. An awareness of Paulo's perspective could have prevented the tension and created a more harmonious work environment.

Getting the Conversation Started

1. What qualities make someone a leader?
2. What attributes make a leader worth following, and which do you admire most in good leaders?
3. What leadership style do you prefer?
4. Who is a leader you aspire to be like and why?
5. Who was the most inspiring leader you have met, and what made them inspiring?
6. Do you see yourself as a leader? Why or why not?
7. What factors influence the relationship between leaders and followers?
8. What are some lessons that you have learned recently from a leader–follower relationship that you are in?

Professional and Organizational Leadership

9. What are the expectations of subordinates, and what are the boundaries regarding leaders asking for favors from them?
10. How appropriate is it for employers to make requests outside of regular office hours, and how do employees typically handle such requests?
11. Can employers request non–work-related tasks from employees, and is it considered appropriate?
12. How should employees handle their leaders continuously assigning them tasks that seem unimportant to the organization's success?
13. When is it appropriate for employees to ask clarifying questions or discuss potential issues like lack of expertise, resources, or time when given tasks by a leader?
14. Are you comfortable with disagreeing with your employer? Under what circumstances is this acceptable?
15. What impact would disagreeing with your employer (or employee) have on the relationship you have with them?
16. What is an effective approach for a leader to solicit opinions from their direct reports?
17. Is the leader primarily there to assist the team, or is the team's purpose to aid the leader? What's your perspective on this?

Deirdre, the leader of a large international team in the Arabian Gulf, recently discovered through a survey that her employees feared her. This revelation came as a shock to Deirdre, who had been in her position for about five years. Upon further investigation, she found that her team felt intimidated by her behavior, which included comparing team members, challenging their results, asking numerous questions, and undermining their contributions in front of top management.

Deirdre realized that the team's cultural dynamic had changed over the years, and the employees, who initially had a strong Power/Fear worldview, now felt empowered to voice their concerns. Understanding the different worldviews within her team enabled Deirdre to move forward and build unity and trust among her team members.

Digging Deeper
Cultural Leadership

18. How do you become a leader in your community?
19. Who are the primary role models in your community?
20. Is being a leader a privilege for a few select people or can anyone become leader? Why or why not?
21. Are leaders always right in your culture? Why or why not?
22. To what extent would you disagree with a community leader? Why or why not?
23. In what contexts are you a leader and in which ones are you a follower? How easy is it for you to switch back and forth between those contexts?
24. How would you recommend someone whose leadership has been rooted in their position go about developing consensus-based leadership?
25. How does leadership differ in various contexts, such as family, work, or community?
26. What qualities do effective leaders in your community possess?
27. How do leaders in your community handle conflicts or disagreements?
28. Are leaders in your community typically appointed or elected? How does this process work?
29. What role does tradition play in selecting leaders in your community?

30. How do leaders in your community stay connected with the needs and concerns of the people they lead?
31. In what ways can leadership be both empowering and limiting in your community?
32. What strategies can aspiring leaders employ to gain support and trust from their community members?

Good vs. Bad Leadership

33. What qualities define a good or bad leader in your community?
34. Which leadership roles are typically trustworthy and which are viewed with suspicion, and why?
35. Would you continue working for a bad leader if your financial situation allowed it? How would your decision differ if your income depended on the job?
36. What distinguishes good followers from bad ones, and how do their behaviors impact leadership?
37. Is it possible for a bad leader to be removed from their position, and if so, how would that typically be done?
38. What character traits or behaviors would make for a good leader but be bad for a follower and vice versa?

"The use of intercultural agility can be applied to relationships between teachers and students to allow for increased understanding and less confrontation, as well as be used to create a space where students can approach their teacher for assistance. The benefits of intercultural agility are in significant abundance and are not limited to any one area of life. It is this adaptability that makes it so useful and necessary in modern society."

—Ahmed Msuya

CONFLICT AND RESTORATION

To err is human, to forgive divine

Tensions were high in a multinational organization not so long ago. Ongoing friction within a Ghanaian team consisting of a male leader and two female subordinates had reached its peak, and it was slowly becoming more evident to all involved that the team's survival was at risk. The leader claimed that a member of his team was being defiant, while his subordinate insisted that, despite her respectful tone and culturally appropriate approach, he failed to take her suggestions into consideration to the detriment of the team and the organization. Something would have to be done before the palpable friction cost the team and the organization more than they could stand to lose.

In a world where every person you meet is a unique cultural individual with differing world views and opinions about various aspects of life, disagreements and friction are inevitable. According to B.W. Tuckman6, even the most effective organizations have a "storming" phase (a stage characterized by high levels of conflict and tension) as part of their team development process. Conflict can make it incredibly difficult for an organization to reach its goals; for a family to live together in harmony; for a community to thrive, so the conflict itself should never be where our stories end.

Victor, the coordinator of several teams within this multinational organization, stepped in to help this team overcome their communication challenges, and resolve the conflict. While he and the subordinate were willing to engage in the process of leveraging the conflict into a growth opportunity for the team, the leader was not. So, Victor's attempts to rebuild trust between them failed, and the team never did realize its full potential.

Getting the Conversation Started

1. When you feel wronged, what is the first thing you do and why?
2. What could people say and/or do to repair wrongs and relationships?
3. What is the best way to express an apology?
4. If there is an issue, do you work to solve it, or do you ignore it?
5. Is conflict better handled directly or indirectly? Why do you say so?
6. Why is admitting wrong and apologizing important (or not important) in conflict resolution?
7. Has your view of the role and process of conflict and restoration evolved over time and if so, how?
8. How does your community view conflict?

---

6 Tuckman, B. W. (1965). Developmental sequence in small groups. Psychological Bulletin, 63(6), 384–399.

9. What is a culturally appropriate way to express frustration with others?

Conflict in Group/Family Contexts

10. How is restoration done if there is a conflict between two families? What about between two family members?
11. Should conflict be resolved in the open or kept private? Why?
12. Which types of conflicts should be handled in the open and which must be handled behind closed doors?
13. What behavior would you expect from a person who has an opposing view to yours?
    a. How does your family handle conflict?
    b. Does this reflect the social norms around you?
    c. What works well or does not work well with this?
14. How does your extended family solve conflicts?
15. How does your company handle conflict with employees or customers? Is it the same?
    a. Does this reflect the social norms?
    b. What works well or does not work well with this?
16. Which is easier to say: "I am sorry," or "I forgive you"? Why is that one easier for you to say than the other?

"People of differing perspectives are vying to be recognized and have a voice on the world stage. This often brings chaos, instability, and conflict, as the world has failed to develop intercultural awareness as it globalized and so barriers have been formed rather than bridges. Intercultural Agility can begin to lead the way to bridging the gap caused by diverse opinions. Through application of IA (Intercultural Agility), people learn to work together toward an inclusive solution."

—Diane McGhee

It had been three weeks since Sudanese businessman, Jameel, had lost his temper on a video call with his Swiss colleague, Hans. Jameel had found Hans too pragmatic and confrontational, adding that he was too task focused, and didn't respect Sudanese culture. Hans admits that he was abrupt during their video call, and that he had put the task over taking the time to get to know Jameel and build rapport. Shortly after the call, Jameel sent Hans a rather rude email, to which Hans did not reply.

There are a plethora of factors and dynamics at play when culturally unique individuals come together with the aim of reaching a common goal. When conflict arises between people, as it inevitably does, using intercultural agility to identify the roots of the conflict helps build understanding. This can leverage that conflict into a crucible in which strong trust relationships are formed.

When three weeks had passed, Jameel wrote Hans another email, apologizing for what he had said and how he had behaved during the video call. Hans immediately initiated another video call to accept Jameel's apology. They then had a good conversation and the tension was resolved.

Jameel and Hans's story shows that we can experience richness on the other side of conflict if we seek resolution more than we seek our own way. The clashes and disagreements we have with others can be used to refine our expectations. When conflict is well-managed, it has the potential to unite a team, a family, a community, or organization in ways we never thought possible.

Digging Deeper

17. How do cultural differences cause conflict?
18. Would discussing cultural differences or cultural similarities bring people closer?
19. How can conflict best be avoided?

Justice and Restoration

20. What does justice mean to you?
21. What impact does someone's power over you have in a conflict?
22. If there were a community court in your community, how would issues be dealt with?
23. Under what circumstances might it be appropriate for third-party mediators to help with conflict or resolution? What would that be like?
24. When an individual has a different opinion than a leader of a group, should they speak up in a group setting, or should they bring it up quietly behind-the-scenes? Does their status, age, or gender matter?
25. When there are issues of mistrust between conflicting parties (including family members), what practical steps could be taken to build trust, and bring healing or restoration?
26. What does forgiveness look like?
27. Some cultures say, "apology requested" and "apology accepted." What does that mean to you?
28. What is the best way to express an apology?

Emotions in Conflict

29. Can you separate the emotional from rational in issues? What is helpful or unhelpful about this ability in conflict?
30. Who is allowed to show anger and who is not? Why?
31. In which situations is it more or less appropriate to show anger or frustration?
32. Which emotions are appropriate to show in public?
33. In the culture you grew up in, what are some long-standing conflicts that haven't been resolved?
34. What for you is the most challenging conflict you've experienced. Were you able to overcome it and how?

ACHIEVEMENT AND ACCOMPLISHMENT

How Do You Celebrate Success?

Irene was in a bit of a bind. She worked for a European company based in a Middle Eastern country. As the Director of Human Resources, she was in charge of developing a reward program for employees who displayed excellent achievement and commitment. She suspected that following the company reward policy of giving a bottle of wine, could offend her Muslim coworkers, but was it worth the pushback from her superiors to deviate from the norm?

One of the best ways to motivate a group of people and build synergy is to reward success, and deciding how that is done is an important step during the formation of the group.

People's views on how to celebrate differ, not only from region to region and culture to culture but also from person to person. Being a keen observer during the initial stages of team formation will allow you to ask pertinent questions and, ultimately, determine the best way for your unique group to recognize achievements. These agreed-upon methods of celebration and reward will be key in creating a safe cultural space where everyone in the group can thrive no matter where they are from.

Irene bit the bullet and decided to meet with her Nordic superiors to discuss her apprehension in giving wine as a reward for loyalty in the predominantly Muslim context. She added that she observed a culture of eating out among people in the city, and there were many popular eating places in malls. She then suggested that staff be rewarded with vouchers to dinners, discounts or memberships to high value loyalty programs, and movie tickets. Despite their surprise that wine would not be accepted as a gift (and to their credit) her superiors allowed her to proceed with her suggestion.

It takes courage to deviate from organizational, personal, and social norms to find new celebratory norms that will be valued by all members of the team. Little is lost when we sacrifice our own way for the benefit of building something for the good of many. The effect that celebration has in uniting a team is multiplied when each member values the means of reward.

Get the Conversation Started
Community

1. How is recognition shown in your culture?
2. Is recognition important in your culture? How is this demonstrated in your culture?
3. What is more appreciated in your community—status or accomplishment?
4. What would be considered "healthy" achievements?
5. Does greater achievement or accomplishment mean that you have a higher social standing?

6. What is considered a significant achievement in the community in which you grew up?
    a. How would that kind of achievement be rewarded?
7. When accomplishment is celebrated, does reward involve a physical object?
    a. What objects are common rewards?
8. Are any goals or pursuits passed down from one generation to another?
9. What are some examples of rewarding individual and group accomplishments?
10. Is it acceptable to show your neighbors and community how successful you are?
11. How far should people be willing to go to achieve their goals?
12. Are there any measures to achieve success that are frowned upon in your community?
13. How does society perceive people who haven't achieved much individually, but have contributed to or facilitated the success of others?
14. If you achieve success, are there certain things expected of you by people around you (colleagues, family, friends, etc.)?
15. Are there certain accomplishments that make you better suited for a future life partner?
16. Are certain pursuits higher in approval ranking than others and are these pursuits similar for both men and women?
17. How is the pursuit of achievement taught to children (at home, in school and in society)?

Work

18. If you produce twice as much as any other colleague, how do you expect to be rewarded?

19. Would you hire someone with more steady experience, or someone with less experience and a short, impressive track record?
20. If your colleague gets a promotion because their sibling is the boss, is this acceptable to you?

To some, achievement may be based only on the quiet success of the work done, while to others, giving recognition is the only way to show that something great has been accomplished.

Edward works for a British company based in India. The Indian branch of the company was very successful throughout the year, so, as expected, the branch was allotted bonus checks for its employees. What Edward did not expect, however, was the disagreement between the British and Indian managers on the best way to give out the rewards.

There are some who believe that only pursuits that benefit the organization as a whole should be encouraged, and little regard should be given to reaching personal goals and self-actualization. Others may realize that as people improve themselves, they will, in turn, improve the organization. It should also be noted that some groups of people would find it offensive to reward subordinates without rewarding their managers or leaders, even if they outperformed their superiors.

Instead of deciding what to do on his own, Edward decided to set up an awards committee that consisted mostly of local managers to match the demographic of the workforce. After much deliberation, the committee recommended that the bonus funds be allocated to the entire unit based on seniority, as opposed to giving the funds to the strongest contributors to the unit's success. This was well received, not only because the committee reflected the views of the majority of the workforce but also (and potentially more importantly) because it preserves the honor of every employee in the unit.

Digging Deeper

21. How does your family celebrate your accomplishments?
22. How do you personally celebrate success or achievements?
23. Do your family's accomplishments influence the way you must live your life?
24. What personal or family accomplishment are you most proud of?
25. What behaviors do you adopt to show someone recognition?
26. In what ways are you encouraged to reward others?
27. What would you most like to accomplish and be recognized for? What do you hope your children will accomplish and be known for?
28. Do you value words and actions of appreciation for constant achievement?
29. What is your motivator to reach an accomplishment?
30. Are your goals primarily externally or internally motivated?
31. Is it acceptable to pursue your personal goals without taking your family's ideals into consideration?
32. What are examples of moral, ethical, and religious boundaries that need to be adhered to when you pursue your ambitions?

CHANGE

How and why do we adapt?

There are few things in life more certain than change. Though many of our days are comprised of routines we may find mundane, we are still guaranteed that things will change. Nothing stays the same. Seasons change. Children grow. Companies gain and lose capacity as markets fluctuate. The global village in which we live and work is becoming increasingly transient with people coming and leaving. Even things established a long time ago, and things that will stand the test of time, will grow, develop, and evolve. Change is inevitable.

The state of flux in which we live requires us to be more agile in our interactions with others at the risk of being left behind in an ever-changing and unforgiving world.

Maybe you're like Stefano who moved to India for work. Stefano wrestled with the rigidity of his own worldview in the first few months of living in a culture that was completely different to his own.

His initial understanding of the new culture led him to believe that qualities he valued such as, honesty, open communication, participation, innovation, and teamwork were absent in his interactions with his new colleagues. The situation escalated to the point where he did not like anyone at work because of these perceived differences, and his frustration grew as the situation did not change.

Getting the Conversation Started:
How Change Impacts You

1. Is change good or bad or neutral? Why?
2. How do you react to change in general?
3. What's your view of change and how do you usually manage it when it occurs?
4. What framework do you use to decide whether a change is good or not?
5. If a change is bad, what redeems it or makes it a good thing to pursue?
6. What are the key ingredients necessary for bringing people with you through change successfully?
7. What does your weekly life look like? Do you have the same routines each week, or are your activities more varied? Why is that?

Personal Change

8. At what speed do you embrace adapting to change?
9. What aspects of life should never change?
10. How best can you handle an unfavorable change to your advantage?
11. Do you find that people overreact to change or underreact? Why do you say so?

12. How important is it for you to change?
13. What do you value more: continuity and stability, or change and creativity? Why?
14. What was the most difficult transition in your life, why do you think it was so hard?
15. What is the hardest part of change for you?
16. Is your society changing in the right or wrong ways? How so?

"There is a global 25-40% failure rate for senior expat assignments and tons of money lost in misconducted mergers/deals/etc. every year. Both cases present a huge loss to companies, which can be avoided by equipping the parties involved with Intercultural Agility. Furthermore, corporations desiring to bring their product to a new market be more successful if intercultural agility was part of their DNA. As Peter Drucker says: 'Culture eats strategy for breakfast'.

—Enrico Werner

Like Stefano, David (who was originally from a western country), started a job in the east. Initially, he too wrestled with the perceived lack of honesty, indirect communication, and team spirit among his coworkers.

After spending some time in a culture vastly different to their own, both Stefano and David began to understand the differing worldviews at play. As they changed their attitudes and perceptions, they were able to build stronger relationships in their new cultural setting. And despite the difficulties and challenges of adapting to a new culture, David found the reward of stronger connections with the people around him far outweighed the comfort of sticking to his worldview.

Furthermore, as Stefano began to learn the culture of his new counterparts, he realized that he needed to change his expectations to improve the situation. His intercultural agility allowed him to see that the expression of the characteristics he valued was not limited to his worldview and past experiences.

Digging Deeper
Work

17. Who in your team is always open to change and who struggles to accept it?
18. How did your company handle the changes and challenges that occurred during Covid? Did you approve of these changes?
19. How do you view different countries' responses to the changes caused by Covid? How did that compare to your country?

Family

20. In your childhood, did your parents change jobs often? How did that affect you?
21. How have activities around holidays and religious festivities changed over the years?
22. In some cultures, the "keeper of tradition" is seen as the most honorable person. Is that true of your culture, and how do they ensure tradition is maintained?
23. How would a dramatic job change be received by your family?
24. Is international travel encouraged in your family? Why or why not?
25. How would your family respond if you chose to live and work abroad?
26. How does your family show their approval (or disapproval) of a life change you make?
27. How did you and your family manage the changes that were brought about during Covid?

Culture

28. How does change affect culture?
29. To what extent is cultural change acceptable or a "good thing"? Why?
30. Does your culture treat change as a positive or negative thing? Why do you say so?
31. What could be considered barriers to cultural change?
32. In what ways does your culture and upbringing affect your ability to change?

DECISION-MAKING
How do you make decisions?

Adrian didn't realize how relational decision-making could be until he had to close a deal with a family business in Dubai. His business supplies training that helps organizations drive sales. When his friend Simone offered to join him for his proposal meeting, he couldn't understand why someone who had nothing to do with the agreement needed to attend.

Adrian approached the meeting thinking that when you transparently present the client with all the facts, they can make an informed decision. He then created an excellent proposal, loaded with reasons why his business was the best choice. He did not consider, however, that there could be other factors that the clients could consider when making their decision.

Decisions are not made in a void. When choosing the best course of action, cultural perceptions and past experiences impact decision-making. Some people even have the voices of friends and family members weighing in, heavily influencing the choice. While for others, the only considerations when deciding are the rules and parameters around that particular decision. So, ask yourself, do rules or trust and relationship drive your decision-making process?

While Adrian's friend Simone was completely unrelated to Adrian's business, she knew the clients very well. Adrian realized that he would not have even been considered for a second meeting if Simone hadn't been there. She brought the "trust factor." So, Adrian invited her to the second meeting as well. He found it slightly disconcerting that she kept interjecting with further explanations and reasons why the potential clients should choose his offer. Simone's unusual approach understood that beyond building a clear understanding of the proposal Adrian was making, the brothers wanted to know that Adrian was someone who could be trusted. What Adrian viewed as interjections or interruptions, the clients viewed as valuable reasons to trust him and consider choosing his business. The brothers didn't know Adrian, so having Simone convince them of the goodness of his proposal made them trust him.

Adrian admitted that he would not have fared as well in building rapport with the clients if he had gone on his own. He admitted that following the rules, sticking to direct communication and keeping things formal (because this is business) would not have put his business in a good position when the client needed to make their decision. What Adrian did not understand was that, for some, a pre-existing relationship is pivotal to decision-making, so having his friend Simone with him helped him garner favor with the client.

Getting the Conversation Started

Personal Decisions

1. Do you share your thoughts with other people when you make decisions, or do you prefer to make them alone? Why?
2. Are personal decisions made by the individual? Are family and friends involved in personal decision-making?
3. How does youth or age difference influence your perceived ability to make decisions?
4. How would you respond to someone who was unable to handle the consequences of their decision after they had ignored your advice?
5. Are there cultural traditions and protocols that impact decision making processes?

Big Decisions

6. How do you make important decisions in your life? How was this shaped by the way that you saw others in your life make decisions?
7. Are there important decisions where the whole community gets involved and what process is followed to make that happen?
8. Are there decisions in life that are best made by people in authority over you (who to marry, what to study, where to live etc.)? Why?

The ripple effects of decisions are far-reaching, so it is important to have a humble attitude in communicating the chosen outcome, understanding the impact our words have.

Boris recently had a difficult conversation with an employee. The employees had previously requested special reconsideration for a significant financial policy in their organization. Though the benefit was not available to him, he hoped it would be awarded to him by virtue of relationship and hierarchy.

The organization operates in a mostly rules-oriented decision-making framework. Understanding this, Boris told the employee that his request for special treatment had been denied. Boris knew that previous requests for exemption hadn't been well received so he took a different approach.

Though Boris could have communicated to the employee in a direct manner, being clear and decisive in letting him know that the benefit would not be awarded, he chose instead to come alongside the employee and communicate with him with the respect that the employee expected.

"I'm so sorry," Boris said to the employee, "The organization values you, but we don't have the funds available to make an exception. There are other people who are in a similar situation, yet they cannot be exempted either. This would create disparity in the organization" Boris continued to note that he understood that the employee had a different view than the organization, and then finally asked how the employee felt after hearing the disappointing news.

Surprisingly, the employee said that he understood that the policy was there for a reason and that he understood that finances were limited. The employee was able to share the personal reasons why he had requested the benefit to begin with. They were even able to reach common ground despite the situation.

Instead of trying to explain things or defend the organization's side, Boris was able to connect with the employee and see beyond the decision he'd had to make. This helped the employee to see that, though rules had to be followed in making a decision, he was valued by the organization.

We cannot neglect the delivery of our decision. Though we may be convinced that we have made the best decision for our family, community or company, communicating that without respect and empowerment could lead to conflict and a disdain for our choice.

"IA guides someone to understand the personal, cultural, and relational dynamics in the room. IA leads us to seek to understand BEFORE seeking to be understood. IA helps decision-makers strengthen their awareness and understanding of the people they serve. IA sees everyone as individual and with unique needs and ways of understanding the world around them and the need of others."

—Jim Foster

Digging Deeper
Decisions in Families

9. Who is involved in group decisions in your family?
10. Who makes the major decisions in a typical family in your society (the father, the mother, an older sibling, a grandparent)?
11. How did your parents divide decision making responsibilities for your family?
12. Should personal decisions be made individually or in community? Why?
13. If a decision is made that shames the family, how is that communicated?
14. In a private family setting is disagreement permitted? How does that influence the way conversations are managed?
15. Describe a situation(s) where your personal preferences and the preferences of your family were not aligned.
16. How does gender influence how you can contribute to a decision-making conversation in your family?
17. How would you describe the process of when someone in your family begins making decisions on their own?

Decisions at Work

18. Who should be involved in group decisions at work and why?
19. Are there certain decisions or announcements that must be made face-to-face? How would you communicate to a staff member that he/she is fired?
20. If you are in a business meeting with a client with your boss, are there certain protocols that will dictate how/when you can contribute to the conversation?
21. How does a leader gather the information/opinions they need to make a decision?
22. If you have a different opinion from your team leader on a subject, is there a culturally appropriate way for you to communicate your viewpoint?

Communicating Decisions

23. What does clear communication look like to you?
24. What is the importance of the communication method in decision making?
25. How do you talk about a decision before it is made? How do you communicate a decision after it is made?
26. How should confrontation be approached when you are angry with a decision?
27. In what ways are positive and negative emotions communicated and what communication channels are acceptable for either negative or positive emotions?
28. How does your supervisor/boss communicate decisions?
29. What style of communication does your supervisor/boss use according to their cultural background?
30. How does your boss's style of communication impact you?
31. Is your supervisor/boss more rational or emotional? How does that affect you?

32. Is your supervisor/boss more direct or indirect? How does that affect you?
33. How is being in public disagreement with someone else perceived in your culture?

ETHICS AND MORALITY
What determines right and wrong?

If everybody does the right thing, we'll all get along, right? Well, it's not that simple. Every person in the world has a unique culture and perception of the world, so, at times, it may be impossible to agree about what is "right".

Even experts in ethical theories cannot agree that there is one way to determine if something is right or wrong. According to some ethical theories[7], the most correct actions are those that benefit the largest number of people. So, an action is deemed good if its consequences are good. Other theories assert that your actions can only be right if you have followed the rules to the letter, no matter who is involved.

Take Lukas and his boss, for instance. While working for a Bangladeshi company, Lukas encountered grossly unethical business practices. Months had passed and the employer had

[7] Bonde, S., et al. (2013). A Framework for Making Ethical Decisions. 2-3.
https://www.brown.edu/academics/science-and-technology-studies/framework-making-ethical-decisions

not paid salaries to any lower-level employees. Since everyone but Lukas was from the same area of Bangladesh as the CEO, they were too scared to confront him about this unethical behavior. Things came to a head and Lukas decided to stand up to his boss and demand that the overdue salaries be paid in full. Unfortunately, the confrontation did nothing to reverse the unethical behavior. It only resulted in Lukas feeling forced to resign, and a deeper wedge being driven between the CEO and his employees, pushing any possible restoration off the table. Nothing can be done to repair the trust that is broken when employees are subject to unethical behavior against which they have no recourse. Looking back, Lukas recognized that beneath the surface of the unethical behavior were power-fear dynamics between the CEO and the staff. In retrospect, he would have brought in a prominent societal figure with more power and influence than the CEO to expose the illegal actions and ensure fair treatment for all the staff.

Getting the Conversation Started

1. Why are ethics important in culture?
2. What are some ethical standards that you believe all cultures hold?
3. Do you have a strict moral code? Why do you hold to that?
4. Is morality culturally determined or individually determined? Why do you think so?
5. Honesty and Legality
6. To what extent do "white lies" exist in your culture?
7. What is an example of when it is acceptable to tell a white lie?
8. When is it acceptable to break the law?
9. What's the difference between legality and morality? Which one is more important?

Instilling Ethics

10. How do you teach your kids ethics?
11. How are ethics and morals taught by those around you?
12. Who is involved in the process of teaching ethics and morals?
13. What behaviors prove that you are ethical and which ones show you aren't?
14. Where do your ethics or morality come from? Where did you learn them originally?
15. What is the role of education in transferring ethics and morals?

"At an individual level, Intercultural Agility provides each of us with a deeper understanding of what it means to be human, to accept what is before us without judgement and navigate the various situations we find ourselves within a global world, even if one never leaves their own country."

—Karin Ovari, CEO and Cofounder of Safety Collaborations

Adding to the complexity of ethics and morality, different cultures often prefer some approaches to ethics more than others. In some cultures, seeking honor is more correct than seeking power or innocence. Some cultures prefer direct over indirect communication, because being indirect is sometimes seen as being devious. Similarly, some cultures consider the dignity of the community more important than keeping a single rule. Intercultural agility helps us navigate these murky waters and identify the deeper dynamics at play when the values of others differ from ours.

Furthermore, some believe that they are above the law, never denying that they are wrong, but not having to face the consequences of their actions. We cannot control the decisions and actions of others. It's our responsibility to do the best we can in each situation.

Sarah works in an industry that aims to rescue women from being abused through social ills; women who are put into immoral situations and lifestyles against their will. Intercultural agility is vital to navigate the immense shame barriers that many women feel. Through deep relational connections she is restoring the honor and innocence of the women with whom she interacts. In addition, Sarah has helped the rest of her team understand the cultural orientations at play that affect how ethics and morality are dealt with from culture to culture.

It is a true and sad statement that when good people do nothing, evil runs rampant in society. It's up to us to take our responsibility seriously. It's up to us to use our intercultural agility and intentional questions to understand the moral framework of others so that we can meet them where they are. Then, it is our duty to empower, give dignity and do right by them in every interaction.

Digging Deeper
Ethics in Society and Business

16. Can your ethics or morality change over time? Have yours?
17. If they changed, where did you learn this new standard?
18. In which way does religion play a role in setting the standards and communicating ethics and morality?
19. Which leaders in society are perceived to have high morals and ethics and which leaders are perceived to have low ethics and morals?
20. How is win–lose negotiating viewed in society? Is striking a hard bargain at the expense of the other party applauded or frowned upon?
21. Have any moral and ethical values been undermined (in your community) in recent years and why has this happened?
22. What needs to happen to bring back some of the lost moral and ethical fabric in society?

23. How is receiving bribes and kickbacks perceived where you grew up? What are examples from different spheres of society where these practices might exist?
24. Are ethics classes taught in higher education and what would be examples of degree programs where this is happening?
25. Who are the parties or groups in society that you believe perpetuate immoral or unethical practices and which parties or groups are working together?

The Complexity of Morality

26. Has your experience in life been consistent with the system of ethics and morality you were taught growing up?
27. What is more important, doing what you have been taught is right, or doing what is legally correct?
28. When is it acceptable to choose family over doing what is right?
29. Is it more important to be right or honest or to protect the feelings of another person, even if it means bending the truth?
30. What are examples of the highest virtue in your culture?
31. Is it important to have a shared value system and/or set of beliefs when discussing matters of ethics and morality? If so, what is it, and how do you approach that?
32. How important are morals and ethics compared to achieving high grades in education and what are examples of way students (and their parents) are compromising on their morals to ensure high grades?
33. Is achieving success and being morality or ethics upright connected to each other? What are examples where they are and what are examples where they are not connected?

GESTURES AND NONVERBAL COMMUNICATION

How do you communicate without words?

Words are powerful, but something that holds just as much leverage in the way people interact with one another is that which goes unsaid. Gestures and nonverbal communication are present in every culture and are part of every human interaction, even when words aren't. They communicate powerful and meaningful messages whether we are aware of it or not.

Consider, even today, what you have communicated to those around you without using your words, such as telling your child you're frustrated with them for running late by crossing your arms or tapping your foot; or showing your coworker that you are proud of them just through a nod. It's vital that people are just as careful with what they communicate physically as they do verbally.

Henry learned such a lesson while he was on a business trip in Burkina Faso. He was new to the area, never having traveled to West Africa, or even the continent as a whole. It was an unfamiliar culture, but one that he was excited to experience, even for a few days. Henry was aware that there would be cultural differences, and he tried to be cognizant of that as he traveled the city. Though he tried to respect cultural differences, an inadvertent misstep left him feeling deeply remorseful.

One afternoon while traveling in a van, Henry saw a beautiful moment shared between a mother and her two sons. The boys were being rambunctious, and their mother was smiling at them; it truly was a beautiful moment. Without much thought, Henry lifted his camera to take a few photos of the precious family, but the mother saw him and immediately lifted her arms to shield her sons from the stranger and his camera. Henry felt a pang of shame as he realized the breach of privacy, and he lowered his device as the van drove away.

Unfamiliar with the local customs and inadvertently adopting a tourist's mindset, Henry failed to consider the implications of his actions. Henry learned that it was better to first form a connection with a person, verbally or nonverbally, before using such a strong gesture like pulling out a camera, whether he was familiar with their culture or not.

Getting the Conversation Started
Community

1. How significant is nonverbal communication within your culture?
2. Which specific gesture denotes approval in your culture?
3. In your cultural context, what connotations does pointing at someone carry?

4. Can you provide examples of non-verbal communication facilitated by objects or food within your cultural practices?
5. What unique gestures from your culture might be misunderstood elsewhere in the world?
6. How are whistles or brief tunes utilized in your culture, and what messages do they convey?

Greeting

7. What are the customary ways to acknowledge someone from a distance without verbal communication in your culture?
8. How do traditional greetings differ based on gender in your culture?
9. Are there distinct non-verbal cues or gestures that convey particular meanings during both initial greetings and farewells?
10. How do individuals typically signal for someone to approach or draw nearer non-verbally within your cultural context?

Taboo

11. What gestures are considered obscene or taboo within your cultural norms?
12. How is the act of touching someone of the opposite gender on the shoulder perceived in your cultural context?
13. What are common mistakes in non-verbal communication that individuals from outside your country might inadvertently make?

Henry's experience with his camera is just one of many stories from which valuable lessons can be learned. Sienna, too, was able to gain invaluable knowledge about a new culture through a seemingly innocuous gesture.

At a community gathering, Sienna found herself engaged in conversation with a friend who was of East Asian descent. As her friend described her mother, Sienna spotted a woman in the crowd who fit the description. In a gesture typical of her American upbringing, Sienna pointed to the woman using her index finger. However, she soon realized that her action was inadvertently disrespectful of her friend's mother. Her friend informed Sienna that she should, instead, have gestured with the thumb or used an open hand. Upon learning this, Sienna promptly apologized and adjusted her posture to express respect, partially bowing toward her friend's mother. Fortunately, both her friend and her friend's mother responded with understanding and kindness, gently correcting Sienna without causing her embarrassment. Despite the unintentional offense caused, both parties recognized that Sienna's actions were rooted in a lack of familiarity with their customs rather than any ill intent.

It is a joy to be surrounded by people, experience life with them, and learn to read their what they are communicating even when they aren't saying anything. Henry and Sienna have learned valuable lessons by partaking in experiences with others and undoubtedly will soak up many more. Enjoy the time it takes to learn the customs and norms of new places and people, especially when they are harder to pick up on.

Digging Deeper

14. What are some gestures that convey messages without the need for words?
15. What gestures set individuals apart from the groups they are surrounded by?
16. From your culture, which gestures do you appreciate the most and which ones do you dislike?
17. Can you identify specific gestures that typically indicate people's emotions or feelings?

18. Are there gestures exclusive to interactions with children or adults, and what repercussions might occur if these gestures are confused or mixed up?

Professional

19. How does the choice of meeting location, the arrangement of the venue, and seating preferences serve as forms of non-verbal communication?
20. What specific non-verbal cues are utilized in negotiations to enhance the likelihood of success?
21. What are examples of appropriate non-verbal communication methods, such as the use of emojis in written forms of communication like text messages and emails?
22. Could you explain how non-verbal cues facilitate the management of turn-taking during conversations?

Understanding Each Other

23. When communicating, who is responsible for making sure the message is understood, the sender or receiver?
24. How can one ensure they have interpreted a message in the manner intended by the communicator?
25. Can you provide examples of gestures and non-verbal communication that involve the entire body, such as posture, exiting or entering a room, and standing?
26. How important are the eyes in communication?
27. When verbal and non-verbal cues conflict, how do you address the discrepancy?
28. How often do you notice nonverbal clues that convey underlying emotions?
29. How accurate are you at interpreting nonverbal clues when you notice them?

30. Is silence considered a form of non-verbal communication, and how is it employed? Who is typically authorized to employ silence in communication scenarios?

DIFFERENCES

What happens when people are not the same as you?

Every human is a unique cultural individual. This means that people could be born in the same place and time, culture and language group, and still have different world views. This speaks to the belief that we are all unique, from our DNA to our fingerprints.

While there are infinite differences that exist between people, there are still shared experiences which could be used to connect people and form relationships. Work colleagues could join a football league, students from different continents could play online games together, and movie and book clubs stretch across the world. In many cases, we are willing to put our differences aside to find the one thing that connects us with others, because not many people like to be completely alone.

Differences could be viewed as beautiful expressions of the human spirit, but sadly, these differences can be seen as walls, and keep us separate from other groups. In the most devastating cases, these differences can be used as tools to divide.

Tyron recently attended a training session with other therapists aimed to equip them in facilitating groups of people as they process traumatic memories from their past. The training covered a wide range of material including themes of shame, sexual abuse, and collective racial trauma. Each person in the group had read a book, sat through a lecture, and the expectation was that they would share and process their experiences with racial trauma together, but they didn't.

Perhaps out of fear or being over cautious, the facilitators decided to split the attendees into two groups: white people were in one group, and Black, Indigenous, People of Color (BIPOC) in the other.

After the separate sessions, it was expected that the group would come together and debrief in the large group, but they never did. There was a sense of sadness in the group at the missed opportunity to create a safe space for healing to take place. There was an added despair as it came to light that, even if a discussion had taken place, the presenters were ill equipped to facilitate a potentially constructive conversation.

When the group did get back together after the separate sessions, there was more of an increased felt distance between the two groups than before. Though Tyron went out of his way to try to be tender in his interactions with people from the BIPOC discussion group, it was as if the trauma that they had experienced now stood between them as a chasm that could never be filled.

So, what can be done to close these chasms caused by our focus on differences? Tyron's greatest regret around the experience was that he didn't speak to the facilitators to let them know that he wasn't in favor of separating the group. He felt that he added to the distance by saying nothing to them. Perhaps in seeing that it wasn't accepted, the facilitators would have chosen differently.

Getting the Conversation Started
Fitting in Versus Standing Out

1. In what ways do you intentionally differentiate yourself from your culture or community? And when is it important to do so?
2. Are there certain ages or circumstances in your culture where people normally differentiate themselves from others?
3. What differences do you appreciate most in other people?
4. What differences in others make you uncomfortable?
5. What are some distinct ways that members of your community are considered "different" and why do you think that is?
6. Describe how fashion trends in your country or community are similar or different to western fashion trends. What does it take for an outsider to become part of a group and belong in that group?
7. Who do you consider "different" from you and in what ways?
8. When you were growing up, did you feel like you were free to be yourself and were your unique differences valued? Why or why not?

Working With Differences

9. How much appreciation of diversity is there in your friendship group or work team?
10. What does "celebrating differences" mean to you?
11. What makes someone an outsider in your social or work contexts?

12. If somebody is considered "not normal" in your community, how are they typically described?
13. Are there certain jobs that are not acceptable for certain groups or people in society?

It was the morning of September 12, 2001, and Amira was at the office. It was the day after the terrorist attacks on the World Trade Center in New York and tensions were high. A co-worker came to her desk and asked if she or any member of her family had anything to do with the attacks. The co-worker knew that Amira was born and raised in Saudi Arabia, and, judged that a firm basis for his hurtful, misinformed comment.

There are many times that the differences between people cause hurt. Some verbalize their anger, mistrust, ignorance, or fear in hurtful ways, destroying any chance of unity or coming together. When confronted with these destructive patterns, a choice must be made whether to retaliate or not.

In response to her co-worker's comment, Amira asked him if he was related to Timothy McVeigh who was convicted of a terrorist attack on a government building in Oklahoma. Her co-worker was white and so was Timothy, so Amira felt within her rights to make the same judgement. Enraged, the co-worker walked away, and they never really spoke again after that.

It's hard when hurtful things happen to us or when destructive words are spoken to us. It's difficult to reach out to people, seeking belonging, only to be met with their walls and their reminders that you and they will never be the same. So, what could be done to break down these walls?

Years after this conversation, Amira admitted that her racist comment in response to his was not the best response. She suggested that in retrospect, she should have walked away first, and maybe even spoken to her colleague at a later stage to understand why he had said something so hurtful. Perhaps considering other people's feelings, even in retrospect as

Amira did, could be a way to keep relationships from being broken by differences. At many points in our interactions with others, we may find that we have a choice to make: will we use the differences between us to reinforce the barriers that exist in society, and perhaps in our own perceptions? Or will we use common experiences, both the joys and the woes, to build relationships with people who may be longing for a place to belong?

We express this choice in our words and actions. We express it in our tendency to listen more than we speak, and in our choice to ask questions before we make assumptions.

Building bridges between our differences is not an easy task; it is a colossal feat. However insurmountable it seems, it can be done, one careful, humble, intentional word at a time.

Digging Deeper
Differing abilities

14. Growing up, how were people with differing learning abilities treated in your school? Were they integrated or separated?
15. How are people with mental or physical disabilities included in society and the world of work?
16. If a person has a physical or mental disability, to what extent should they be part of public life?
17. In what ways do religious views impact how mental and physical handicaps are perceived?
18. Is accommodation offered for people who are physically or mentally handicapped in your culture? (sign language interpretation of live speeches, wheelchair access of public buildings and hotels/restaurants, etc.)
19. How accessible does the government of your country make communication for people who speak the minority language?

20. Discuss the factors that contribute to the positive, neutral, or negative vocabulary used to describe people with physical or mental disabilities in your community.

The "Limits" of Differences

21. When does "being different" become a problem in the community?
22. How could someone differentiate themselves in your culture? What do you think of the idea that "Today's 'different' is tomorrow's normal'"?
23. Describe the cultural and racial diversity of your childhood friendship groups.
24. When, if ever, is it acceptable to date or marry someone of a different race or culture?
25. How are different sexual orientations perceived in your culture?
26. In what ways is the younger generation allowed to be different from the older one?
27. Discuss the factors that contribute to the positive, neutral, or negative vocabulary used to describe various sexual orientations in your community.

"Understanding the worldview, beliefs, practices, and culture of people who represent other countries is critical to developing a shared understanding of the challenges we face. With a shared understanding, we will then be able to develop a shared approach to common challenges. Developing an interest in, and inquisitiveness about, other countries and cultures is central to the work we do in developing defense policy abroad. This attitude demonstrates respect for our partners and will often elicit important elements at the heart of our partners' goals and interests. Without such IA, we risk establishing blanket policies that do not account for differences in culture."—Bill Parsons

FOOD

Food, glorious food!

Food is glorious in its variety of tastes and textures, but even more so in its ability to bring people together. Food reveals the hearts of those who prepare it and wins the hearts of those who partake of it. Around tables all over the world, norms of culture, tradition, and etiquette are both observed and neglected as platters are passed around and chatter fills the air. Food is truly glorious!

Part of the complexity around food is that we can be at our most comfortable and most vulnerable around those tables. Those meals do more than give insight into our culture; they reveal our very souls.

When Yasmin and Khalil invited their Malaysian friend Junada over for dinner, they were unsure how the evening would unfold. They had no idea of Junada's food preferences, as they had only known him a short time. They weren't sure they had enough to talk about. You may be familiar with the uncertainty involved in inviting someone of a different culture to your home for a meal. The endless list of things to worry about, from conversation topics, to making sure the house is clean, are enough to make you want to cancel the dinner altogether. At times, the additional layer of culture makes the prospect more stressful than enjoyable.

Despite these concerns, Yasmin and Khalil took the leap and invited Junada to their home. To their delight, the evening turned out to be a great success. As they shared that meal, the conversation smoothly coursed over a variety of topics, deepening their relatively new friendship. Not only were they disarmed by the merriment of the evening, but their friend was too. They were even able to discuss food preferences. Junada politely commented on the meal he had been served and then let them know about what he would enjoy in future. The night ended with Yasmin and Khalil being invited to share a meal at Junada's, and the meals they shared continued for many more months thereafter. It cannot be denied that settings where food is involved are slightly more relaxed and lend themselves to openness and starting good conversations.

Getting the Conversation Started

1. What was the best meal you have ever had? Why was it so special?
2. What was the most significant meal in your childhood, and why did you find it so significant?
3. What is the purpose or function of food?
4. What does food symbolize?

Growing Up

5. What role did food play in your house growing up?
6. Who was involved in making food in your childhood home? Why was this the case?

7. When you grew up, how was throwing away food viewed, has it shifted over the years?
8. In what ways did your parents emphasize or de-emphasize eating nutritiously when you were a child?
9. What types of dishes and recipes are passed on through the generations and how important is it to continue to pass them on to future generations?
10. What are some food-related customs or traditions that are common for significant non-religious events in your community? (e.g. moving into a new house, buying a car, opening a new business)
11. Are there specific foods served during births, reaching a certain age, weddings and funerals? What are they?

Food and Health

12. Which foods are forbidden or taboo to eat?
13. Is there a connection between what you eat and your health?
14. How do people link food to health?
15. How do you create a healthy food culture for yourself and those who live with you?
16. What are some of the food traditions you grew up with that relate to the period of pregnancy and the months following the birth of the child?

Though a lot can be revealed about a culture through food, much more is revealed when we dive in and share a meal together. There is an opportunity in each plate to taste and learn the beauty and complexity of cultures different from your own.

Alfred felt excited to be part of a gathering of influential leaders by a provincial ruler in the Arabian Gulf. Twenty-five people had been invited, and he was the only westerner. The evening's proceedings had been explained to him: there would be some conversation, a time of prayer, and then a meal would be served. Already out of his depth, Alfred was surprised to find that all the other invitees spoke little to no English. That would make for quite a challenging night. He struggled to share his thoughts with the other guests as he spoke no Arabic, so he resorted to conversing with one of the servers whose English was better than that of the guests. Being able to communicate in English made the evening feel more enjoyable, and Alfred began to build rapport with the server as the various courses of the evening meal were served.

When the host saw them speaking, he strongly reprimanded the server and then pulled Alfred aside. When Alfred tried to defend the server, the host was adamant that they should not speak. The host viewed speaking to the server as disrespect and felt dishonored by it.

It would have been easy to shrug off the host's words as harsh, but Alfred saw what was happening beneath the surface. The disrespect that the host felt came from a deeply rooted worldview. As a guest, it would stand Alfred in good stead with his hosts if he honored the protocols during the meal to which he was invited. Though he didn't speak to the server for the remainder of the evening, he wondered if his actions would result in never being invited to such an event again.

Food is more than just an aspect of culture. It is a window to our hearts. Sharing a meal can stir emotions and bring back memories, it can uphold tradition and break down barriers. The food we share not only nourishes and heals, but it also binds us together if we are willing to be vulnerable, learn, and share.

It was Louise O. Fresco who said, "Food. . . in our own tradition, is something holy. It's not about nutrients and calories. It's about sharing. It's about honesty. It's about identity." The key is in the sharing. It is in our sharing that we learn and humbly impart what we know to others. It is in our sharing that we grow together, break down walls and make room for ever deepening relationships.

Digging Deeper
Current Food Habits / Social Food Habits

17. Who makes the food in your house currently? Why is this the case?
18. What is the role of food in relationships? (Family, Friends, Work)
19. What is common practice when it comes to dealing with leftovers?
20. How does food play a role in showing generosity (if at all) and does it differ depending on who you are showing generosity to?
21. Does food play a role in building relationships at work, and what would be examples of common practices in the work context?
22. How often is it appropriate to eat out (at a restaurant), and why do you believe it to be so?
23. Who is typically invited to join you or your family for a special meal (friends, family, colleagues, etc.)?
24. What role does food play in family-gathering traditions?

Food and Beliefs

25. What is the significance of food in your community? Why is it deemed so important or unimportant?
26. What are some examples of religious festivals in the calendar where food plays a role?
27. Is it important that you take care of your body by eating certain types of food from specific sources for any of the following reasons: ethical, spiritual, cognitive, religious, social, longevity, health, financial?

28. What are foods that are believed to have healing powers or effects? Why is that?
29. What are some benefits of trying food from other cultures?
30. With the trichotomy between eating for health, comfort, or fellowship, what do you see as the balanced intersection?
31. How are modern food habits different from traditional ones in your community?
32. Give an example of what a traditional meal would consist of in your community?
33. How is being overweight viewed and has this view shifted in the last two generations?

FRIENDSHIP

How Do We Build the Ties That Bind Us?

Friendship, one of the great joys of life. To know a dear friend for many years, and even the companionship of someone new, is something that touches us deeply.

Navigating cross-cultural friendship can be difficult. A unique challenge is posed, as you cannot hide behind the safe wall of "professionality" or "acquaintanceship", where the established relationship has a clear title and only has to go so far. Once you start peeling away the layers of a person, you learn more about them, but are also increasing your need for cultural sensitivity due to their vulnerability.

People find their friends in different places. For some, beautiful friendships are formed through work, colleagues turn confidant. For others, professional relationships have their place, but true friendship comes from other parts of life, like community groups and social clubs.

For Henry, community within the workplace was proving difficult to create. He led a team in the United States and had several staff from other parts of the world. In efforts to build trust with his team member Geteye, who was from Kenya, Henry chatted with him occasionally over coffee where they discussed life as well as job performance updates. Geteye vocalized that he was having trouble connecting with people in the area, and Henry, having been trying to build relationship with Geteye for a while, asked what he could do differently to grow their relationship.

To both Henry and Geteye, work was a place where they made meaningful friendships and welcomed coworkers into their personal lives. Culturally, however, they had different ways of doing this.

Geteye's response to Henry's question about friendship was powerful, "When you want to build community, you schedule a coffee with me weekly. We put it in the calendar, start on time and end 60 minutes later. You message me on WhatsApp and ask how I am doing. That is helpful, indeed. . . When I want to build community, you and I go to the farm and over time we pick the berries, we dry them out, get the beans, sort the beans, roast the beans. . . then we choose our coffee, our mugs, and the place, and have an unhurried conversation. If we don't like the coffee, we go back to the farm and this time with our families. To build community, we do life together."

After hearing this, Henry and Geteye were able to unpack some of their cultural differences. As a result, they began spending more unhurried time together and Henry noticed an improvement not only in his relationship with Geteye but also improvement in Geteye's morale, connection at work, and even in his job performance.

Friendship and human connection are not things to put on pause. They add value to our day-to-day lives and help motivate us. Life finds meaning when it is shared with others.

Getting the Conversation Started
Forming Friendships

1. Are your friendships based on common interests or with people you have context with?
2. What is the spark that creates a connection with someone who eventually becomes a friend?
3. Do you have a large group of friends, or do you prefer a smaller circle?
4. Do you have a childhood best friend?
5. Can friendships be developed freely or are there community rules that guide friendships?
6. What is the trait you look for in a friend above all others?

Building Friendships

7. What happens first—building trust or building relationship? How do these two work together?
8. What is your favorite way to spend time with your friends?
9. How much time do you spend with friends?
10. How long does a friendship last?
11. If you are not in close physical contact with someone, what is the expectation for a friendship over a distance?

Friendship & Family

12. Do close personal friends become "part of the family"?
13. Would you consider your closest friendships to be with family or people outside of your family?
14. What does it mean to be a good friend?
15. Do your parents and extended family have an interest in getting to know your friends?
16. Do you introduce your close friends to your family?
17. Are your friends invited to family functions like weddings and holidays?

Noelle was in a similarly difficult, yet eye-opening situation as she pursued friendship with Amari during the pandemic in 2020. The women had a relationship over WhatsApp video chat as language learning partners. They connected naturally, loved chatting and both desired to eventually spend time together meeting in person. Amari, a Syrian woman, invited Noelle to her home for a meal, a natural next step in their budding friendship. Noelle was thrilled at the invitation but had to decline Amari due to Covid-19 visitation restrictions from the program she was with. She knew she needed to follow the restriction rules but was upset at having to tell Amari "no." Every week, Amari continued to invite Noelle to her home to eat and every week Noelle would profusely apologize and explain why she could not come.

At the start, this cycle of inviting and declining was putting obvious strain on their relationship and Noelle felt Amari begin to shrink back and close off in their conversations. The weeks went by, they continued their virtual chats—Amari continued to invite, Noelle politely declined, and slowly, Amari cooled towards her friend and opened-up again. Noelle could sense Amari's disappointment and also noticed that she was understanding.

Noelle was perplexed at the repeated invitations but knew there was a deeper cultural current that she was missing. She later learned that Middle Easterners will often give vague, yet positive and face-saving responses to an invitation even when they know they can't or won't make it. Rather than giving a "clear" reason, they will often say something about maybe going, God-willing, and then it's a gamble whether they will show up. Amari was not sure how true Noelle was in her responses, so she continued to invite her over for a meal on the off chance she would say yes.

Noelle felt stuck in this situation. She had no way to accept Amari's invitation, no matter how badly she wanted to. She later learned she could have beat Amari to her end-of-chat-invitation by broaching the subject first, exclaiming how excited she was to come eat with Amari and her family! But only after the pandemic, when visitation was allowed again.

Asking questions, the right ones anyway, does not often come naturally. It requires effort and practice to do well. Had Noelle started a conversation about hospitality with Amari, she could have received some much-needed insight and found a way through the situation she was in.

Digging Deeper
Closeness

18. How is friendship defined in your culture?
19. Who were your closest friends growing up and why?
20. Do you consider close family members as friends?
21. How does one deepen a friendship?
22. How are friendships different at different stages of life?

Differences

23. Are you comfortable and free to make friends who are different from you (background, ethnicity, etc.)?
24. Who was your most different friend and why?
25. What was the most challenging friendship you have been part of and why?
26. How are friendships influenced by culture and gender?

27. Are friendships between people of the opposite gender common? Are they socially acceptable?

Entanglements

28. What are the cultural and societal expectations of deep friendships (like calling on for help during crisis)?
29. A common saying is that "a friend in need, is a friend indeed." Should a friend be obligated or expected to help a "friend in need"?
30. Is there a role for friendship in career advancement and if so, how does it work?

RELAXATION AND FREE TIME

How do you relax and have fun?

Cultural background, natural tendencies, and familial ties all play a role in a person's definition of relaxation. Cultures that are fast-paced and work-oriented are often full of people who view time used to relax, work on hobbies, and even see friends and family as something to be "carved out" of their prioritized work routine. There are other cultures that view work/life balance differently and "work to live" rather than "live to work."

For Tonya, the latter was the case. While she worked a corporate job, her lines between professional and private time were thin, and she was happy to welcome coworkers and even subordinates into her daily life, which she preferred to keep rather relaxed. Tonya was a team lead and had to let an employee know that it was time for them to take retirement status, some uncomfortable and often unwelcome news to give. She decided she would take Michael out for an afternoon coffee to chat and catch up and deliver the news at the end of their conversation. However, this choice of delivery method was not well received, something that took Tonya by surprise.

When she broke the news to Michael, his frustration was not as much about the news itself but more about the way it was delivered. He was happy to enjoy some "real" time with Tonya, separate from work matters, and felt the time was spoiled by discussing work, especially his looming retirement.

For Michael, any time spent outside of the office building he considered time to "relax," whereas Tonya looked for ways to incorporate "relaxation" even into her time at work. Because of their different understanding of free-time, each ended up hurting the other—Michael was hurt because of his false perception of Tonya's care for their relationship and Tonya was hurt by Michael's poor reaction to her attempt to show him kindness.

Had one of them slowed for a moment to attempt to reconcile in their mind the reason for the other's actions, they may have been spared the misunderstanding.

Getting the Conversation Started
Vacation

1. How often does your family vacation together?
2. Do you consider "sitting" to be lazy and a waste of free time?
3. Are rest and recreation a priority for your family and community?
4. What are the usual relaxation activities of people across ages in your community?
5. What would be your perfect relaxation activity if time and money were unlimited?

6. Does your community create opportunities for members to spend their free time together through events and community activities?

Free time

7. How do you define "relaxation"?
8. Is the idea of relaxation different in different cultures?
9. What does "rest" look like for you?
10. How does rest differ from relaxation?
11. Do you value having free time to relax, or would you prefer more time to work?
12. Do you enjoy spending free time with others or by yourself?
13. If you typically relax with people, do you prefer to relax with family or friends?
14. How do you decide what to do with your free time? Do you make a plan or keep your options open?

But to the preference of most, relaxation is not to be muddled with work. And the Johannes family know how they like to spend theirs.

The area they live in affords many outdoor opportunities and because of this, they take full advantage—often traveling with friends and family to the desert or beach for a holiday. Their ideal camping spot is secluded, and with the feeling of being untouched, yet to be discovered.

While driving out to their destination, the Johannes family passes stretches of desert open to the public packed with vacationing families, all in tents placed close together. These vacationers enjoy long evenings of barbeques, music and story-telling all together, making new friends and taking in the social atmosphere. For many, this is what they picture when it's time to enjoy recreation.

But the Johannes's pass-by and watch with smiles out the car window as they head to their perfect destination, somewhere a bit quieter and with not as many neighbors! Relaxation and free time have their own role in each culture, a beautiful thing to explore when getting to know somewhere new.

Digging Deeper
Time off at work

15. In some company cultures, applying for your annual leave is seen as a lack of commitment to the company. Do you agree or disagree?
16. What activities are typical for a family at the end of a workday and during the weekend?
17. Is relaxation more about being active or being pampered/served?
18. How do you teach your kids the importance of relaxation and having free time?
19. Do you have consistent relaxation time set aside as a family?
20. In your culture and community, what do children consider relaxing and restful?
21. Do you think recreational activities can become future careers? If so, what are some examples?
22. Are certain recreational activities associated with societal standing, castes, ethnic groups, etc.?

Bonding through relaxation

23. Does watching a movie count as bonding time?
24. Do you think it is important to vacation by yourself and prioritize self-care?
25. How much sleep is too much?

26. When you have had a long and stressful week, what activities refresh and renew you?
27. If people spend money on free time and relaxation, what is considered "normal" and what is considered extravagant?
28. How much vacation time off would you prefer to have in a year? How much time is "too much"?
29. How do relaxation and free time differ across genders?
30. Are certain relaxation activities considered female-only activities? Are some considered male-only?

MONEY, STUFF, AND WEALTH

How do you regard your earthly possessions?

While some strive to increase their financial gain in pursuit of a better life, others shy away from money, claiming that it is the source of many of life's problems or even the root of evil itself. Certain groups believe wealth is synonymous with power and prosperity, diligence and ingenuity, but others view prosperity in a less glamorous light, linking it to selfishness, pride, and greed.

Tensions can rise when money, wealth, and prosperity are perceived in conflicting ways. Craig, a business owner living in South Asia, learned an important lesson when he needed to collect a debt from a local businessman who had borrowed money from him. Despite the businessman having ample funds, he had failed to repay his debt for an extended period.

When dealing with a culture different from your own, it is essential to bear in mind that some people may prioritize contracts and timely debt repayment, while others consider relationships more valuable than money. Consequently, they may place less emphasis on honoring financial commitments promptly. Understanding the cultural values and worldview held by the local man, Craig knew it would not be wise to confront him about the debt directly or publicly.

Instead, he invited the local man to casual meals several times, and over the course of their conversations, Craig subtly mentioned the debt. As anticipated, the businessman eventually paid the debt after one of their many meals together. Through his intercultural agility, Craig successfully navigated a potential conflict. He communicated in a manner that preserved dignity and avoided shame and disrespect.

Getting the Conversation Started
The Purpose of Money

1. What is the purpose of money?
2. You may have heard it said that "less is more." What does this statement mean to you?
3. How is money perceived in your cultural context?
4. What are things that money can and cannot acquire?
5. In your culture, does anything hold greater value than monetary wealth?

Wealth, Status, and Inheritance

6. Do you perceive a correlation between success and wealth? Why or why not?
7. What are some symbols of wealth and status in cultures worldwide?
8. Which possessions, such as watches, handbags, clothes, shoes, homes, or cars represent wealth in your culture?

9. How does money play a role in shaping parts of your culture?
10. Is wealth synonymous with honor in your culture? If yes, what contributes to this perception? If not, what motivates individuals to pursue wealth despite this?
11. Do you find that money equates to power in your culture? Why or why not?
12. How is wealth passed down from generation to generation in your culture?
13. Are you expected to share your wealth with extended family? How do individuals navigate these expectations?
14. Do family members frequently request financial assistance from you?
15. How does culture influence the act of saving money for the future? What are some methods of saving that are specific to your culture?

During his time working as the American liaison at a company in Oman, Robert experienced tension between the American donors' desire for transparent financial reporting, and the Omani leaders' emphasis on trust and respect for their authority. In Western business practices, it is customary to request financial records during negotiations and transactions. However, Robert's familiarity with Middle Eastern culture enabled him to navigate this request delicately, avoiding any suspicion, cynicism, or distrust.

Understanding the importance of maintaining relationships, trust, and transparency in partnerships, Robert communicated his request for financial records indirectly. This approach affirmed the strength of their partnership while addressing the necessity of the financial records for the project. Consequently, he avoided causing offense to any party involved and successfully concluded the business deal. Over the years, Robert honed his ability to balance the needs and expectations of both parties without compromising the objectives of his assignment.

Digging Deeper
Poverty, Wealth, and Generosity

16. To what extent are wealthy individuals expected to be generous in your culture?
17. What is the impact of donating money in your culture, and how is it perceived?
18. How might someone do "good" with money in your culture? What is considered doing "bad" with money?
19. How does your culture perceive individuals who fall into poverty? Is poverty linked to shame or piety?
20. In your culture, who is expected to help those that are living in poverty? Why is this the case?
21. Where do individuals in need of funds for business ventures typically seek loans in your culture? How does the system of interest and repayment operate?
22. Is the practice of paying interest accepted in your culture?
23. How do investors in your culture make profit on their investments?

The Value of Money

24. Do you think that a person's happiness is determined by their wealth? Why or why not?
25. In your culture, is having a substantial amount of money perceived positively or negatively?
26. Is it preferable to display wealth publicly or is it better to keep it private? Why or why not?
27. Which holds greater significance: money or happiness?
28. Do you think wealth management is a common practice for many people?
29. Is the pursuit of wealth a priority for you and your family?

30. Why is it that the rich become wealthier while the poor become poorer? What steps can be taken to maintain a balance?
31. It has been said that the problem with affluent countries is not their wealth but their perception of poverty. To what extent do you agree, and why?

GENEROSITY AND DOING GOOD

Why do good?

Every culture has different ways of sharing goodness, as well as receiving it. It can be a balancing act as a cultural learner, navigating what is acceptable to give and take depending on where you are in the world. Nonetheless, showing kindness and humbly asking questions is universally welcomed.

Johanna was living in a bustling neighborhood in Istanbul, Turkey. She had gotten to know many neighbors in her apartment block, and one of them, named Burak, often extended kindness to her. He had told Johanna that he would be happy to bring packages up to her apartment if she wasn't home to do so herself. One afternoon, a table was delivered to the complex for Johanna, it was large and heavy. Her plan was to bring it up to her apartment later that day with the help of her friend when she got home, but Burak was insistent that he bring the table up for her, which he did.

Johanna proceeded to profusely apologize to Burak, telling him that he really did not have to carry her table up the stairs, he could just leave it, while also throwing in "thanks" and saying that she would somehow pay him back for his help.

Since Johanna had been living in Istanbul for quite some time, she had become familiar with the Turkish concept of "komşuluk," the idea of helping your neighbor. For Burak, leaving the table for Johanna to take care of was never an option, and Johanna knew this. However, in Turkey, you never accept help and leave it at that. You must give many thanks, show your gratitude, sometimes even try to refuse help, and always offer something in return. While that was not Johanna's learned way of giving and receiving help, she had adapted to the way of life in Turkey.

Some may see this situation and not find it to be "generous" at all, because they see generosity as doing something without expecting anything in return. However, that is a one-sided way of looking at a multifaceted concept. Generosity, doing good, kindness—none are black and white. To the Turks, part of receiving kindness is showing gratitude by giving in return.

Getting the Conversation Started
Practicing Generosity

1. How are charity and generosity expected in society?
2. How is generosity typically practiced? Anonymously? Publicly?
3. Can generosity be measured? If so, how?
4. What are some actions that would be considered especially generous?
5. If you receive something in return for doing good, does it count?
6. What is generosity in your culture?

7. Is generosity one of the values typically associated with your culture?
8. Who do you admire as a generous and benevolent person?
   a. What are their characteristics that make them this way?
   b. How do you think they became like this?
9. Is hospitality considered part of generosity? How is it practiced?
10. How is generosity instilled in children, if at all?

Boundaries on Generosity

11. How would you respond if someone was "too" generous to you? What would be considered the appropriate response?
12. Can you be too generous?
13. What is considered the limit of generosity?
14. Is caring for and giving to the poor required in your daily life?
15. Is there a "bad" kind of generosity?
16. Who are the people you typically give to in your life and what form does this giving usually take?
17. Do gifts come with strings attached?
18. When you give a gift to someone do you expect anything from them in return?

While Johanna had a proper understanding of "doing good" in this intercultural interaction, Daniel realized that his intention to "do good" was misplaced.

After working for many years with a refugee relief organization, Daniel had picked up many refugees from the airport and taken them to their accommodations in the city he worked in. On one particular day, he was picking up a young woman who had just arrived from Uganda named Aisha. It was late afternoon; he had not yet eaten lunch and so asked Aisha if she was also hungry and would like to pick up some food on the way to her apartment. Aisha nodded yes and so Daniel stopped at a local café for takeout. He knew very quickly that he had made a mistake.

As he handed her a menu, he could see in her eyes that she was uncomfortable. In an effort to do good by Aisha with a comforting, warm meal after her long journey, he had unintentionally put her in an incredibly uncomfortable situation. This woman, who had likely endured immense hardship, was placed in the middle of a bustling restaurant minutes after arriving alone in a foreign country, given a foreign menu with foreign foods and asked to make a quick decision. What she needed was rest and relief; she was still in shock and not in any position to be unnecessarily surrounded by crowds of people.

After Daniel realized the state of this woman, he immediately offered for her to wait in the car while he ordered the food and she gladly obliged. After bringing Aisha safely to her new apartment, Daniel briefly apologized—choosing to wait until a later date to discuss what happened. Thankfully, he and Aisha are friends to this day and have had a number of opportunities to have healthy and healing dialogue about Aisha's first day in the country.

Digging Deeper
Expectations on generosity

19. Is it okay to expect others to be generous if you are generous?
20. Is it acceptable to be generous to people who are poorer or richer than you?
21. Which types of generosity are considered easier or harder?
22. How easy or difficult is it for you to be on the receiving end of generosity and good deeds?

23. What are typical ways people respond when they receive something beyond their expectations?

Public Displays of Generosity

24. Under what circumstances can generosity be done publicly and when is it expected to be done privately?
25. When is talking about your generosity considered inappropriate? Or when does talking about generosity become linked with pride or arrogance?
26. Would pressure from others affect generosity?

Religion and Giving

27. Is your community more focused on doing "what's right" as perceived by the group or what's right according to some spiritual norms or laws?
28. What does it mean to be "good" in your culture? Which structure determines what is good? (Religion, government, families, etc.)
29. How is generosity practiced? Is it shown in charity (giving to organizations that do good work, e.g., among the poor and sick) or in hospitality?
30. Is generosity required in your religious practice?
31. What type of benevolence is most common and why? Hospitality toward people with less means, giving alms directly to a poor person, giving to a charity (an organization that does good to the poor, society), or giving to a religious organization?
32. Is volunteering common and how is that encouraged?
33. When is generosity expected to be reciprocated? Is it linked to debit and credit in relationships?
34. Are there types of good deeds practiced in society that don't improve the community in the long run?

SOCIAL VALUES

What do you value?

Living by certain morals and values is an integral part of culture. They reflect the ways a culture can change and give valuable insight. They allow for deep connection, as they are often instilled in people from childhood and are as second nature.

Shubum had seen, while working in different parts of China which is not his native homeland, how people in Hong Kong maintain a social value that they hold very closely: privacy, especially compared to other parts of the nation.

He was part of organizing a "working parents' networking activity" where the parents who joined the group were invited to share photos and videos of their family and children. In Mainland China, the initiative was very well received; the working parents were quick to send in their photos and share stories of their children, but in Hong Kong, the networking activity did not go over as expected. No one was sending in media for the activity and Shubum received feedback from a local team member advising him to find a different way to engage this group. He learned that the people of Hong Kong greatly value their privacy and consider family goings on to be incredibly personal, and only to be shared with those deeply connected to the family, not used as a "get-to-know-you."

Shubum knew from then on to consult with a local who was familiar with the cultural customs and social values before implementing new community involvement efforts.

Getting the Conversation Started

1. Do you think social values are mostly the same across all cultures? Why or why not?
2. What are social values that are important and relevant in today's world?
3. Are social values the same for everyone in your community and culture?
4. What are some examples of violating social values?
5. What is a recent example you've experienced of the breakdown of social values in your society and culture?
6. What are ways you have seen initiatives (small or big) rebuild healthy social values?
7. Are certain social values prioritized for females as they become young women? What are these social values?
8. Are certain social values prioritized for males as they become young men? What are these social values?

In the home/family

9. Is hospitality an expectation in your home? Why or why not?
10. What is a social value demonstrated in your family that you appreciated as you grew up?

11. How were you taught to be obedient or "good" as a child? Was counsel from parents or elders an important part of discipline? Was corporal punishment an acceptable form of discipline?
12. How do your daily life choices reflect the values imparted to you by your parents? Have you adopted a different set of values as an adult?
13. What do you believe is the most important value for a person or a family to pursue for a successful life?

Community expectations

14. How does society treat a member who is a good person but behaves differently from what is expected in society?
15. What behaviors show whether someone is a good or bad person?
16. What characteristics does your community value most in a person?
17. What characteristics does your community value most in a company or business?
18. What characteristics does your community value most from community and government leaders?

Friends/acquaintances

19. What societal values were important to your friends growing up?
20. What societal values are valued most by your friends currently?
21. How do you decide who should be welcomed into your circle of friends?
22. Would you be friends with a person if their values were significantly different from yours?

Social values manifest in different sectors of society, especially when people who hold opposing values are working together.

Hannah was an English teacher at an ESL center in Mali. She often formed relationships with her students, who varied in age. At the end of each course, the students took an exam and had to pass to receive certification.

At the conclusion of a particular course, a student did not pass the final exam. The natural next step to Hannah (and the center's policy) was for the student to retake the course, as failing the exam implied that the student's level of English was not proficient. However, the students of the class assembled and came to her, insisting that their classmate pass the exam.

After being trained in Intercultural Agility, Hannah looked back and realized the nuance of the situation she was in; from her perspective as a teacher, giving the student certification did not properly reflect his true ability and was setting him up for failure in his future employment endeavors, on top of the fact that she could be jeopardizing the integrity of the center she worked for. However, from the community perspective, which aligned with an Honor-Shame worldview, the students were defending the honor of their fellow classmate, as failing was considered "shameful." She realized how serious their request was when they even claimed they would go on strike if she didn't pass the student (in Mali, protests and strikes are prevalent throughout the workplace, schools and society).

Hannah wanted the ESL center to remain "Innocent" and the students wanted their classmate to maintain "Honor."

Ultimately, Hannah decided to follow the center's policy and insisted that the student would need to retake the course and pass in order to receive certification. While the students were not pleased, Hannah ensured the ESL center remained a qualified institution. It is difficult to say what the "right" or "wrong" decision was for Hannah, because there wasn't one. There were colliding worldviews that she needed to answer to, caught in the crossfires of a delicate intercultural scenario. The agile way forward was to discuss with the students and come to a mutual understanding by creating a third cultural space.

When a community has alignment over shared values, it has unity and can progress. When values are not shared, there is room for opposition and hostility. Asking questions to address what goes unsaid allows for a space to be formed where people are comfortable and encouraged to share that which they hold close to them.

Digging Deeper
Personal

23. What societal values, when followed, give a person status?
24. If you are living outside your home culture, what social values are shared between your culture and your host culture?
25. What are the main social values in your culture?
26. Which ones do you value the most?
27. How do you teach and share social values with your children?
28. What are some of the ways someone can violate social values? How does this affect the community?

Societal institutions

29. How does the government instill and enforce the values that are important to the government?
30. What is the role of education in instilling social values?
31. Are there groups/tribes/subcultures in society that focus on different social values?

"With Intercultural Agility, a marketer can identify the unique blend of motivating values that their audience shares and can understand how those values influence deeper needs. IA gives a marketer the skills to craft messages that maximize on the social values of an audience rather than simply trying to focus only on the solution being presented. In this way, instead of having tunnel vision, a marketer can effectively and holistically build a relationship with their audience based on a much more genuine understanding of their values."

—Caleb Strauss

EDUCATION

What Does Education Look Like Across Cultures?

Rona, a student from Nigeria at a foreign university, was attending classes to help improve her English. Her instructors, who preferred an interactive approach to learning, found her to be distant and withdrawn in class. She was not benefiting from the lessons and her language skills were not improving. They wanted to help Rona and were open to using other methods but were having difficulty finding a way to reach Rona because she didn't participate in class. They weren't sure what was to blame: the language barrier or a deeper relational issue. This led not only to frustration, but a stalemate—they were at an impasse and needed to find a solution to continue moving Rona's education forward.

The experience of Rona and her instructors is not unique. Educators and students often have trouble connecting because they both come from unique cultural backgrounds and have different ways of relating and delivering educational material. The classroom, from elementary to university level, is full of intercultural relationships that require cultural awareness to be productive and successful. So how did Rona's instructors get to the root of the issue?

Rona's teachers decided to sit down with her in a less formal and quieter environment and simply ask questions, getting to know her story. The conversation naturally led Rona to share her reservations and fears about class. What they learned was powerful; she felt she was not qualified to speak up in class and that she compared poorly to her peers. She was crippled with fear when answering even the most basic questions.

At the beginning of this conversation with Rona, another obstacle became apparent. Rona's accent was so overpowering that her instructors continually had to ask her to repeat herself, an intimidating request that became obviously shameful, and naturally led Rona to shut down. Fortunately, the teachers were language instructors, and they were determined to understand the cause of the difficulty. They asked Rona to type answers to questions on a keyboard and discovered that she was switching the letters "R" and "L", making many of her words almost unintelligible. They learned she was not cold or dismissive at all, just lost in the complexity of the English language. Knowing the cause of Rona's language difficulties made it possible for the teachers to address Rona's learning needs. After meeting with her instructors a few more times, Rona viewed them as friends and opened up to them more deeply. This newfound comfort and familiarity, as well as receiving personalized help with her pronunciation, bled into the classroom, where Rona started to be more engaging and receptive. Her language skills improved.

Rona's success story began with the interculturally agile approach of her teachers. They were open and curious and approached Rona's difficulties in a personal and culturally intelligent way. It all started with asking right, culturally agile questions, which led to the building of trust in the student/teacher relationship. When trust is built, educators have a chance to engage their students at a deeper level and design educational pathways that are most successful for them.

Getting the Conversation Started
About Educational Upbringing

1. Can you share with me about your learning journey?
2. What did you study at school, and do you find it prepared you for what came next?
3. What would you change about the way you were educated?
4. What was valued most in your school by students?
5. What was valued most by teachers?
6. Do you find higher education or skill training more practical or beneficial?
7. What is more valuable—formal or informal education?
8. What was the grading system like in your schools?
9. Did you find it to be equitable?

For Teachers

10. What do parents hope for when it comes to the educational pursuits of their children?
11. Do you find that students value receiving an education?
12. Is higher education after secondary school an expectation from parents?
13. What kind of extracurricular education might children engage in? Sports? Arts? Music? Other?
14. Is it acceptable to engage in free and open discussion and debate within the classroom or are students expected to absorb material from lecturer, without conversation?

15. What freedom do students have to question or disagree with their teachers?
16. In cultures that values formal education, how can or should the importance of informal education be raised?
17. What does the future look like for home schooling children or self-taught professionals?
18. How valuable is textbook learning? Do you see it offering more than life experiences?
19. Should creativity be encouraged in education?
20. To what extent should an emphasis be placed on rote learning and memorization?
21. To what extent should problem solving be taught in school?
22. What is discipline like in schools for children in your community? Are there punishments and rewards?
23. Are there schoolwide/city/state/national standards for testing or achievement?
24. What makes someone qualified to be a teacher?
25. Are teachers typically male or female?

While some instructors unexpectedly face cultural challenges, others work in a multicultural environment where receiving students from different backgrounds is the norm, and it can be all too easy to make false generalizations about students based on where they come from.

This was the case for Hannah, who worked at an international school in Australia. At the beginning of each year, she received her class list and excitedly looked at the names and nationalities of her new pupils. She loved the diverse environment she got to dive into each day, but Hannah knew that she was making assumptions about what a student would be like or how they would behave in class based on where they came from. On the one hand, she felt this helped her prepare in advance what techniques and styles she would use to engage all of her students and curate a learning environment suitable to them. However, the preconceived notions before she even met her students, whether positive or negative, did not amount to any sort of success.

Every young student, while it's likely they will have picked up on cultural norms from their nationality, is developing their own unique personal culture, different from that of their parents and siblings. They see the world in a way that is special to them and will be receptive to different teaching styles and tactics not simply because of what their home country dictates, but because they are a uniquely wired cultural human being.

Hannah's efforts to plan ahead are valiant, but she is missing out on special dynamics she could have in her classroom if she is placing stereotypes on her pupils. When introduced to the Three Colors of Worldview, a tool that brings awareness to people's different cultural drivers and cues, Hannah discovered a new approach to teaching and connecting with her students, one where she didn't have to assume anything. Instead, while planning different activities to help students engage in class, she can ask three simple questions, getting to the heart of all different worldviews. Does this activity bring and preserve honor to the student, or will it induce shame? Does it do right by the student and allow them to maintain a sense of justice, or will it create guilt? Does it empower the student, or does it make them feel fear? As Hannah remains cognizant of honor, innocence, and power with her students in the classroom, she will be able to stop playing the guessing game and implement measures that work.

Students of high school age, while they may be the most sociable and outgoing of us all, can be the most difficult to connect with because their culture is so unique and doesn't have a place for people who don't understand it. For this reason, it's common for teachers to have an inability to connect with their students, breeding an environment ripe for contempt.

Jacob, during his freshman year of high school, was sitting in his last class of the day, eager for the dismissal bell to ring. His teacher was giving final remarks and issuing the instructions for their homework that evening when Jacob noticed a discrepancy in the instructions. He did what he normally would, bring to light what was confusing about the assignment and ask for some clarification; it was close to the bell after all, and everyone wanted to get out on time, he figured even the teacher. However, Jacob did not expect what happened next. His teacher perceived the question as a correction and a disrespectful challenge to their authority; the teacher refused to amend the mistake, nor provide further clarification. Jacob, frustrated that he had been misunderstood and becoming defensive, chose to argue further. This created enough tension that he was asked to leave the classroom.

No teacher who willingly chose their profession would want to have strained relationships with their students that create a hostile learning environment. So why do we see situations like the one between Jacob and his teacher? It boils down to different views of power and hierarchy as well as having different understandings of context. While Jacob was used to having teachers who ascribe to a very low power distance, it seems that this teacher did not fit the same mold, and Jacob had not picked up on that. Had Jacob phrased his question differently, pointing out that he wanted to do well on the assignment out of respect for his teacher, rather than bringing to light an error, he may have been able to save face on both ends. Culture varies drastically person-to-person, even between those who come from the same nationality, which is something we often neglect.

Education is powerful. It is foundational. It has changed the ways of the world. Asking the right questions will help you turn educational settings into a place of intercultural agility, where students of all ages can thrive.

Below are questions to start conversations about learning and education from an intercultural perspective and to help facilitate conversations between teachers and parents/students, broadening perspectives.

Digging Deeper

26. What is the role of education in your society?
27. Is education necessary for a society? Why or why not?
28. What was your parents' connotation when they talked about education and what did that communicate to you about their worldview?
29. Is education equally necessary for both genders in your culture?
30. What is the expected level of education for boys and for girls?
31. What do you hope for the educational future of your own children?
32. What role does or should religion play in education?
33. What do you feel religious education is like?

Education and Status

34. Does your culture correlate level of education with status?
35. What are the social connotations between public and private education?
36. Is continuing education acceptable for adults?
37. In higher education settings, how important is hierarchy, especially between students and professors?
38. Is there military education or training in your community?
39. What is training like for tradespeople?
40. What does continuing education look like for tradespeople?

41. What education do you look for when you hire?
42. How are educators valued and well paid in society?
43. What level of status do teachers have?
44. In what ways is education seen as uniquely respected status?

"The need for an intercultural agility course at the University level is both urgent and growing. Increasing the intercultural agility of university staff and faculty as well as international students would supplement the university through equipping faculty and staff to achieve greater productivity in their interactions with international students, maintaining and strengthening relationships with international stakeholders, and increasing the revenue from expanding international student enrollment."

—Charissa Deen

GENDER ROLES

Do our differences divide or strengthen?

If there is an aspect of culture marked by generalizations and stereotypes, gender roles would be at the top of the list. Add to that the unspoken and unmet expectations surrounding gender, and we have a history marred with assumptions and bias.

Throughout history we have seen tension around varying ideas about what roles gender should fulfil in society, and what happens when people step outside of them. Whether it is different generations or different geographic cultures, often when approaching someone with differing ideas around gender roles, the tendency has been to assume that they are wrong, and their ideas are either "destructive" or "oppressive." Add to that the complexity and nuances of culture, and all the empowerment and disempowerment that go with that, and we quickly realize that there is much to learn in this area if we are to move forward with healthy views of gender roles.

Take, for instance, the team of Romanian engineers visiting a branch of their multinational company in the Philippines. As many of the Romanian staff had not traveled extensively, this trip was one of their first cross cultural experiences, so there were some social nuances they were unaware of. While the Romanian staff spent time with their Filipino counterparts, observing the day-to-day operations of the branch, they observed an issue that they felt needed immediate reporting to the company's HR department as they believed they had identified a case of abuse of gender roles. They had observed that the young woman was providing meals for the executive staff, all of whom were male, and they felt the need to report this as a matter of urgency.

Too often, the tensions between gender roles lead to divisive assumptions. Reporting the matter to HR would have resulted in consequences for the employees involved and created tension between the Filipino employees.

Stefan, the leader of the Romanian contingent, investigated the matter before it was brought to the HR department. In the end, he discovered that the female employee had asked her colleagues to try her food to help her improve her cooking skills. Furthermore, Stefan found that the executives had all contributed toward the cost of the ingredients.

Stefan asked questions; he dug deeper to understand this situation instead of making assumptions based on gender roles. His colleagues' assumptions could have caused a division between the company employees, but thanks to his intercultural agility, a potential conflict was avoided.

Getting the Conversation Started

1. In your culture, who is typically considered the head of the household, the father (male figure) or the mother (female figure)?

2. What types of societal expectations do men and women have placed on them in your culture? For example, are women expected to handle domestic duties such as cooking, cleaning, and child-rearing, while men are expected to work outside the home?
3. What are your thoughts on a man staying home to look after the children and manage household responsibilities while the woman works? Do you agree or disagree with this idea, and why?
4. Does your spouse work? If not, was this a choice, or are there other factors at play?
5. How do members of your family, including husbands and sons, contribute to domestic chores and responsibilities?
6. To what extent are women allowed to work outside the home in your culture?
7. According to your cultural norms, are there specific jobs or professions that are traditionally associated with men or women?
8. How much do gender differences play a role in matters of inheritance and ownership in your culture?
9. What are the significant phases or milestones in a woman's life according to your cultural traditions and beliefs?
10. Similarly, what are the important phases or milestones in a man's life?
11. In what ways and settings are men and women allowed to interact in society according to your cultural norms?
12. To what extent are platonic friendships between men and women socially acceptable in your culture?
13. What are the specific roles and responsibilities of grandmothers, mothers, aunts, and sisters in your society?
14. Conversely, what are the specific roles and responsibilities of grandfathers, fathers, uncles, and brothers in your society?
15. Is it common for men and women to eat together in your culture, and do they typically eat at the same time?

16. Are there places that are designated for either men or women exclusively? If so, how do these spaces differ from one another?

Work related

17. How do you make men and women feel equally included whenever you ask for volunteers to manage a project or delegate an important task?
18. To what extent do you believe that men and women should receive equal pay for equal work in the workplace?
19. Under what circumstances do you think it is acceptable for a woman to manage a team or supervise men in a professional setting?

Debbie Ford describes self-awareness as "the ability to take an honest look at your life without any attachment to it being right or wrong." Perception management is a tool that facilitates self-awareness and self-management. Managing personal perceptions is an excellent way to navigate complex intercultural interactions, including ones where tensions exist between genders. One tool that KnowledgeWorkx uses to help us learn how to slow down our assumptions is called DIR. By going through the process of "Describe," "Interpret," and "Respond", our brain is forced to slow down. As a result, we can avoid jumping to conclusions. The DIR model empowers us with strategies that by slowing down conversations lower the influence of personal biases in a situation. The model also helps make responses less emotional in the heat of difficult situations.

Saskia was embroiled in such a situation. A male colleague was being rude and aggressive with her, being demanding and controlling in his communication with her without letting her speak. When this occurred for the third time, Saskia had a choice to make.

She could have brushed her colleague off as another stereotypical male and avoided the conflict altogether. Alternatively, she could have confronted him head-on, challenging his behavior, but she chose neither of these options.

She chose instead to have a sit-down conversation with him where she informed him that she did not appreciate the way he spoke to her. She went on to explain that though this style of communication may have worked for him in his past employment, it did not match the organizational culture they were trying to build within the company. Using DIR, Saskia was able to remove the emotional reactions from the conversation. She was, instead, clear about the facts of the situation in a calm manner. She ended her piece by asking him how he suggested that they could build a better working relationship going forward.

Though her colleague was initially defensive and unwilling to listen, Saskia's final question disarmed him and drew him in to engage about the working relationship. After their open conversation, they moved forward as male and female colleagues with a third culture space in which to work together.

Digging Deeper
Growing up

20. What did adults around you assume about you because of your gender growing up?
21. In your family, who was responsible for performing routine tasks around the house, such as doing the dishes, cleaning, or fetching water, especially in a rural setting?
22. In what ways are boys and girls treated differently in your culture?

23. In what ways do you treat young children differently because of their gender?
24. Are there any associations between cleanliness or uncleanliness and gender in your culture?
25. Is there a preference for having a boy or a girl baby in your culture? If so, what are the reasons behind this preference?
26. Challenging and Accepting Gender Roles
27. In what ways do you think your parents mirrored the expected gender roles of their culture and in what ways did they act contrary to those expectations or norms?
28. What limits does your culture put on your gender that you think are beneficial for your welfare and well-being? Conversely, are there any restrictions put on you that are not beneficial?
29. How do you address situations where either gender assumes the role of a victim to avoid their responsibilities?
30. How do you address and rectify misconceptions that others may have about the treatment of different genders in your culture?
31. What are some gender-based taboos prevalent in your culture?
32. To what extent should respect for culture and values make way for the acceptance of differing sexual orientations?
33. What are the primary concerns or fears faced by women in your society?
34. What are the significant concerns or fears experienced by men in your society?
35. What are the topics that men are more likely to discuss exclusively with other men?
36. What are the subjects that women are more inclined to discuss solely with other women?

MUSIC, FILM, ART AND EXPRESSION

How do you express creativity?

The term "culture" embodies a duality in its definitions. While culture can denote the expression and appreciation of art, KnowledgeWorkx defines culture as "The sum total of our thinking, speaking, and acting," encapsulating the impact individuals or groups have on their surroundings. These definitions intersect as art often serves as a crystallization and reflection of an individual's or group's unique cultural identity. Additionally, art can challenge and reshape societal ideas and norms as individuals interact and engage with it.

The depth and complexity of these expressions are limitless, making art in all its forms a feast for the senses that fills the soul. The beauty in its variety reflects the beauty of each unique cultural individual. Take music, for instance. It plays a role in the worship of some, while others abstain from playing music to show their devoutness. Music and film are used to stir emotion, inspire, and even make socio-political statements. It is undeniable that the arts have the power to move people and shape culture.

Adeline's work as a photojournalist often required that she travel to cultures quite different from her own. Her role on these trips was to photograph specific aspects of life in those places to encourage financial donors to respond when they saw the results. As she became more interculturally agile, however, Adeline began to feel that her instructions not only limited her creatively, but often forced her to capture images that had the potential to rob people of their dignity and present a limited understanding of their culture. After coming to this revelation, Adeline worked very intentionally to ensure that she maintained that delicate balance: ensuring the pictures she took resonated with the client's mandate as her Innocence / Guilt worldview would have her do, while empowering and honoring those whose pictures she took.

Getting the Conversation Started

1. Does art matter? Why or why not?
2. How do you define art, and do you believe it is constrained by any factors?
3. What do you think is the importance of art in society and how should it be expressed?
4. Could you share your favorite movie with me, and what makes it personally significant to you?
5. When was the last time you encountered a piece of art that deeply moved you, and what about it evoked such emotions?
6. Do you think modern music is losing the cultural values it once had? If so, why do you believe this is happening?

7. Is there a universally accepted method of artistic expression, and are there forms of expression that are frowned upon?
8. In your community, how are individuals encouraged to express themselves through art in all its forms?
9. Are there street musicians in your area, and how are they perceived by the community? Do people typically stop to listen or offer financial support, and why do you think they are regarded in that manner?
10. When it comes to music, films, and art, do you believe there should be censorship, or should there be complete freedom of expression? What are your reasons for holding this viewpoint?

Expression and Culture

11. How do you personally express yourself?
12. How do music, film, and art bring different cultures together?
13. What role does music play in shaping cultural identity?
14. How does the music in your community reflect your culture? In what ways is it similar or different from the music of other cultures you've encountered?
15. What difference would it make to the world if more people supported the arts?
16. Are there particular genres or styles of music from other cultures that you feel a connection to?
17. Should art classes such as drawing, painting, or sculpting be included in K-12 school curricula? What are your reasons for supporting or opposing their inclusion?

> *"Cultural competency education will engage students, faculty, and staff at our university in development that will prepare them to live and work in the diverse world. Intercultural Agility will help guide us to analyze intercultural dynamics and develop strategies for adaptation in our recitals, concerts, dramatic productions, and exhibits. IA has the potential to transform the way the institution responds to and embraces issues of diversity."*
>
> —Elaine Pauw

Scott, his wife, and another American couple were invited to join some Azerbaijani friends for dinner one night while they were staying in Côte d'Ivoire. It started as an enjoyable evening despite the language barrier, and the group spent much of the night gathered around a wood-fired oven making small pizzas. Scott and his wife enjoyed the pizza making process and asked the host if they could take pictures—the host quickly agreed. As they sat down to eat dinner, the host returned and politely asked them to delete the pictures they had taken.

Scott was usually very careful about taking pictures—especially in intercultural situations. For some reason, he let his guard down that night and got caught up in the moment, not grasping the enormity of the situation for the Azerbaijani men: even though they were living in a foreign country, they still feared being found by the police.

The duality of culture is stark in this story. Creating food is an artful expression and sharing that experience with new friends is powerful. While photography was another medium to capture the moments of that special evening, it was up to the artist to discern when their expression was appropriate. There are times when the means of creative expression we are most comfortable with may be different from another's. In those times, we need to pause and consider how to respond in ways that uphold the honor, innocence, and empowerment to those around us.

Careers in Art and Music

18. Are the arts accessible to everyone, or are they typically reserved for the talented few?
19. What music styles are prominent in your community?
20. How do artists typically generate income? Is it through patronage, sponsorship deals, ticket sales, or sales of books/records?
21. In your culture, would pursuing a career as an artist bring honor or shame to your family? What are the reasons behind this perception?
22. In your society, how does the income of successful artists (such as writers, musicians, and actors) compare to that of individuals in other professions (like doctors, engineers, and politicians)? What factors contribute to this discrepancy?

History of Art and Music

23. How has music in your society evolved in the past few decades? In what ways has it remained unchanged?
24. Similarly, how has art in your society changed over the past few decades, and in what ways has it remained consistent?
25. What are the preferred music styles among different generations in your culture, and are these styles indigenous to your culture?
26. What music styles are unique to your culture?
27. Are music classes included in the K-12 school curriculum in your culture? If so, why do you believe children are typically taught to play instruments or sing?

Arts and Religion

28. How do music and religion intersect in your culture, if at all?
29. In what ways can music, film, and art be incorporated into worship practices?

SPORTS AND EXERCISE

Why do you work out?

"Hashim Amla... Dale Steyn!" the vendor exclaimed to some very pleasantly surprised shoppers stopping by his stall in the souk.

Annika and Ryan were visiting Dubai for a weekend getaway and had stopped in a shop selling local jewelry and gemstones. The stall attendant, after greeting them, asked where they were from. Upon hearing their home country was South Africa, he replied, "Baie mooi" which translates from Afrikaans to "very beautiful." He then began naming South African cricket players to the smiling couple. Soon learning that the souk clerk was Pakistani, Ryan surprised him by naming off Pakistani cricket players, like Babar Azam and Shaid Afridi. All three were radiating excitement from the connection they had just made, faces beaming. It was so refreshing to be in a conversation with someone from such a different culture, but unexpectedly have so much on which to connect.

A love of sports is a common human experience, shared by many cultures. In the Latin world, football is a passion Latinos share, whereas in the United States, football is a completely different game, but still invokes the same level of passion from its fans. While the game may change, one thing remains true: Sports brings people together. Even across continents, sports create a connection that transcends culture and language.

Getting the Conversation Started

1. Are sports an important part of the community in your culture?
2. How have sports impacted or shaped your community's culture?
3. What is the role of successful athletes or sports celebrities?
4. Are there certain people or groups in society who are expected to play sports? Are there certain groups who are expected to not play sports?
5. Are there societal or educational benefits for those who are good at sports?
6. What forms of exercise are encouraged in your culture?
7. Is there a place for exercise or sports in the work context? What are some examples?
8. How are nonphysical sports viewed (either mental games like chess or computer/online games)?
9. Does your country or city have climate or environmental conditions that influenced what sports were important and common?
10. How does your community view sport on the global stage?

Youth/childhood

11. How important is Sports in schools? Are sport and exercise prioritized in schools?

12. Are there certain sports that are encouraged to begin at a certain age? Is this true for girls and boys?
13. How important is it to introduce sports to children at a young age in your culture?
14. How is PE (Physical Education) viewed in education, specifically by gender? Is it viewed differently for girls and boys?
15. Were you physically active growing up?

Community

16. Are rivalries between different teams common?
17. Are school teams cheered on by the entire community?
18. How do people view pursuing a career in sports?
19. Is exercise a priority for the elder members of your community?
20. Is there a difference in how the older generation and the younger generation views exercise and in which way has the level of engagement shifted?
21. How serious is the community about time around sports?
22. Is there a connection between sports and level of income, status, and ethnic background?
23. Is community identity tied to the success of a sports team?

Amy took up a new sport later on in her life: running. She loved everything about it, the challenge, the endurance, and especially the community. There was a "running friend group" in her neighborhood that she joined where the women could share victories and struggles that they faced while training.

The expected response to these vulnerable messages was a word of encouragement, maybe small bits of advice here and there or a "here's-what-worked-for-me."

There was one woman in the group chat who frustrated Amy with her replies to Amy's messages. Rather than sharing encouragement, this woman, who was from a different culture than Amy, would give very long instructional answers, explaining what Amy needed to change in her workouts, diets, routines, etc.

While it was likely that Amy's friend was offering advice in good faith, especially since she was a seasoned ultrarunner, it was not the friendly encouragement that Amy wanted or needed. But, with a few questions and a little bit of humility, these women, despite their cultural differences in offering advice, were able to connect over their love of running.

Digging Deeper
Personal

24. Do you have a longstanding relationship with any sports teams? Why?
25. What is your favorite sport and your favorite team?
26. How do you prefer to exercise?
27. What are your favorite individual and group sports?
28. Do you play any sports? Why or why not?
29. Have you ever felt the need to learn a sport because it is part of a culture that interests you?
30. What level of emphasis did your family place on sports? How did that impact you?
31. Is it important that you take care of your body by exercising for any of the following reasons (spiritual, mental, religious, social, longevity, health, financial)?
32. What are considered to be the benefits of sports in your culture?
33. What sports or exercise activities are still practiced in your culture today that point back to old traditions or practices?

Gender

34. How much are women to be involved in sporting activities in your culture?
35. Are certain sports viewed differently for different genders?
36. Are women in your society encouraged to swim and are swimming costumes for women considered to be too revealing?
37. In which way does gender play a role in what is acceptable or not acceptable in sport?

HUMANS AND NATURE

How Should We Engage Nature?

There is a delicate and beautiful symbiotic relationship between humankind and nature. Poets have penned verses in praise of natural wonders, while painters have adorned canvases with the beauty and splendor of living things. Though humanity has created layers of separation between itself and the natural world, an innate appreciation for nature's beauty and wonder remains.

Santosh and his family moved into a twelve-story apartment building with a courtyard in the middle of the grounds. Constructed a few years prior to Santosh's arrival, the building's playground had fallen into disrepair, and residents had taken to discarding trash over their balconies onto the courtyard and play area. As a result, children had stopped playing there, and the outdoor area was seldom used.

While there is some consensus about mankind's responsibility toward the planet, there exists a plethora of ideas about how to care for it, with differing views often influenced by cultural factors. Some cultures, closely intertwined with nature and reliant on its resources, fiercely protect it, while others more distant from nature may appear indifferent to opportunities to mitigate environmental impact.

One day, armed with gloves and garbage bags, Santosh and his family embarked on a mission to clean up the courtyard. Initially, the neighbors were indifferent, but after some time, their curiosity was piqued. While the family's act of cleaning up the common area seemed unusual to most of the people in the building, the cultural tendency to seek honor led some neighbors to join Santosh and his family in their endeavor.

It took little time to clear the area as others joined in. The neighbors even put some money together to repair and paint the playground equipment. The courtyard once again became a place of community where children played and families connected.

Nature surrounds us, influencing us whether we acknowledge it or not. Undeniably, we have made an impact on it. Nature sustains our bodies and feeds our souls. When we desire to return to the purest forms of food, or seek relaxation, we are pointed toward nature in its most natural state. We cannot deny our need for untouched nature, nor ignore opportunities to care for it.

Getting the Conversation Started
Taking care of nature

1. Do you spend time in nature? If so, what activities do you typically engage in?
2. What role did nature play in your upbringing?

3. In your culture, what is the primary purpose of a nature park? Is it primarily for facilitating recreation, providing refuge for plants and animals, or protecting ancient sacred grounds?
4. Was environmental stewardship a prominent theme in the culture in which you were raised?
5. How has your relationship with the natural world evolved from childhood to the present?
6. Can you recall a specific instance when your perspective on your relationship with nature shifted? If so, what prompted this change and how did it occur?
7. How does your connection to the land contribute to your sense of home?
8. Is it possible for someone to have a sense of rootedness without a direct connection to the land?
9. How do you believe the connection between nature and culture should be taught to the younger generation?

An interesting definition of culture is "What humans make of the world." Intriguingly, by that definition, it seems that the opposite of nature is culture. Nature is that which remains untouched and uncreated by humans, while culture encompasses everything humans create, including intangible elements such as relationships and governance. The two are deeply intertwined, and nature plays a significant role in forming and developing human culture.

Basil and his girlfriend, Elaine, decided to visit Waterton Lakes National Park in Canada one long weekend. Initially, they planned to set up a picnic at a popular campground famous for its magnificent views. However, due to the crowded conditions, they decided to walk to a more secluded area. There, they found a tranquil spot with a picturesque view of the lake surrounded by trees. They soon meandered away for a brief stroll with their dog, leaving their belongings between two trees beside the lake.

When they returned from their walk, there was a family nearby wanting to take a picture of the lake and trees from the exact spot where their belongings lay. Frustrated, Elaine questioned whether it was necessary for them to move all their things just so the family could take a photograph. Tension rose as they spoke. The family, hailing from a completely different culture and language, resulted in much of the conversation being lost in translation. Nonetheless, they remained adamant that Basil and Elaine's belongings be removed for their picture.

The celebration of the beauty of nature is expressed in various ways by different cultures. While it would have been easy for Basil and his girlfriend to refuse and request the family to take their picture elsewhere, the family made a valid argument for their request: the land belonged to everyone. After further deliberation, Basil and Elaine moved their belongings so the family could take their picture.

Upon reflection, Basil realized that the differences in how people experience nature are deeply influenced by their worldview. No single expression carries more weight than another. Slowing down our responses and seeking to understand how those worldviews are at play will make room for conversations over confrontation and dialogue over defensiveness.

Digging Deeper
Nature and Religion

10. Do you believe the world is beyond repair, or do you hold to the belief that all things can be made new?
11. Is a restored creation part of your worldview? If so, how do you contribute to the new creation?
12. What is your perception of the human condition?

13. How are nature and spirituality connected in your religious practice?
14. In your society, is there integration between your relationship with nature and your belief system?
15. Can you provide examples of what this integration looks like in practical terms?
16. Importance of Nature and Land
17. Which holds greater importance to you: human life or all life (nature)? Why or why not?
18. Should humans act as stewards of nature (i.e. population control through hunting, game reserves, etc.) or should we seek to allow nature to flourish with as little influence as possible? Why or why not?
19. What are some effective practices from various cultures that you would adopt to promote protection and care of the land?
20. How has the view of nature you were raised with influenced your dietary habits?

THE SPIRITUAL WORLD AND BELIEF IN THE SUPERNATURAL

What do you believe in?

Claire and Michelle were thankful to be on their way home, the unease from the afternoon was still wearing off.

Earlier that day, they had wanted to be somewhere new in preparation for the hours of studying ahead of them, so they drove to a neighboring town for a change of scenery and to be free of distraction. A friend had told them about a renovated historic hotel with a French Quarter theme, so they meandered in and headed to the coffee bar.

There was lots to take-in in terms of architecture and design, but the hotel lobby was strangely empty, not a guest in sight. As the two girls ordered a coffee, the barista became incredibly chatty. She was remarkably friendly, and unasked by the girls, began sharing intimate details of her life. While the barista was still making drinks, another employee came by, but she wasn't wearing a uniform or anything signifying she worked for the hotel. Oddly stoic and quiet, this employee spoke only a few words to the girls, asking if she could take their photograph with a polaroid camera. She exchanged a few words with the barista, and it became clear that she really did work for the hotel. Taken aback, the girls smiled politely and instinctively told her yes, assuming the photograph was for them. The woman smiled and began waving the polaroid as it was developing, mentioning something about how she would be happy to one day tell her grandkids about the "pretty girls she met at the hotel."

At this moment, Michelle began to feel very strange. With the barista sharing intimate details of her life and her photograph now in the hands of a stranger, she suddenly did not want to be in the hotel anymore. The barista however, so excited that they were there, insisted on giving them a tour of the hotel. Smiling and not outwardly showing their hesitation, the girls said yes. The barista took the girls through the gift shop and grand lobby, explaining all of the renovations and history and showed them the upstairs rooms. The longer the girls were inside the hotel, the more uneasy they felt. Neither of them discussed their uneasiness with the other, and neither of them realized that they were both feeling the same way. Each girl was very spiritual, they felt a heavy pit in their chest, believing something was spiritually dark about the place.

Eventually they were left alone to do their studying, but Claire and Michelle did not stay long. When they had a chance to talk and realized they both were feeling the same way, they quickly packed up their things and decided to make the drive back home.

To some, the spiritual world is nothing but a means of explaining away odd encounters, to others, it explains the mysteries of life. Whatever it may be, the spiritual world has a relevant role to play in every culture, some are just more evident than others.

Getting the Conversation Started
Society/Community

1. What is the importance of the supernatural in your culture or society?
2. How important is it to "pray" or request help from an object of worship before you start a new project?
3. What are some examples of good or bad omens (a happening believed to be a sign or warning of some future event) in your society?
4. What is the role of (deceased) ancestors in your society? Do they need to be appeased and kept happy? Do they have the ability to influence the living by bringing blessings or curses?
5. What animals are sacred in society? What animals have supernatural powers (either live animals or animal products)?
6. What are the causes of sickness and accidents? Are they believed to be caused by natural causes or by supernatural causes (or both)? Give examples.
7. Which supernatural practices are "common" in society but actually frowned upon or not talked about in general society?
8. What are some examples of certain actions or rituals that are integrated into significant social events (e.g. birth, marriage, adulthood, opening a business, buying a car)?
9. Are certain spiritual practices connected to special individuals or groups in society?
10. If someone has special privileges or powers related to the supernatural, how are they passed on to other people (i.e., is it "in the family")?

11. To what extent do animistic practices manifest themselves in orthodox religious practices?

Daily life

12. How does the supernatural impact your daily life?
13. Is the spiritual world disconnected from daily life or seen as an integral part of it?
14. Is fate directed by each individual or is it already written?
15. In what ways can humans invoke the intercession of spirit beings in their lives?
16. What rituals or prayers are common at the start of a day, before eating, and before sleeping? Which ones do you practice?
17. How does one ask "god" or "the gods" for guidance/protection?

Ahmed was a man who firmly believed in the supernatural and was keenly aware of its impact on his life. He was the owner of a small store that was very successful. He loved his business and decided that he would venture out and open a second shop in a different location. Full of hope and enthusiasm, Ahmed took a chance and it was paying off; the store was incredibly successful, revenue was streaming in.

However, the success of the store was short-lived. After a few months, he announced to his friend Harib, "I am going to close the store!"

Shocked, Harib asked Ahmed why he would do this when the store was so profitable.

"That is exactly the problem! The sages are convinced somebody has become jealous and the evil eye has been cast. I must close before there is a major loss."

Ahmed was confident that his success would soon come to an end, and he decided to close his store before the evil eye could induce repercussions. His spiritual beliefs intensely impacted his day-to-day life.

Digging Deeper
Personal beliefs

18. To what extent do you believe in the supernatural?
19. Do your actions and beliefs in this life affect the afterlife?
20. Do you believe in miracles?
21. Do ghosts/spirits exist in this world?
22. Do you believe in a power greater than yourself?
23. Do you believe that there are things that cannot be seen but can be felt, such as a sense of who is going to call you before your phone rings?
24. Do you think we are humans having spiritual experiences, or spiritual beings having human experiences?
25. Is there anything beyond this world that we can observe?
26. Have you ever experienced anything you couldn't explain? What was it?
27. What agency do supernatural beings have in the lives of humans?

Growing up

28. How important was the concept of "God (A Higher Power or Being)" in your household growing up?
29. What were you taught to be "afraid of" in the spiritual world?
30. Did your parents teach you about a variety of faiths as a child? Were you able to choose which one to believe or were you expected to believe the same as your family?
31. Were there measures your parents took to safeguard your home from the spiritual world growing up?

FAITH AND RELIGION

Why do you believe what you believe?

They say there are three things never to discuss at a dinner party: money, politics, and religion. Nevertheless, gaining an understanding of the faith of others could deepen the connection and strengthen relationships, if approached with care and respect. Your faith may be very close to your heart, a subject that you regard with value and reverence, while the religion of others may be something you don't really understand, something you may not regard as highly.

While it is true that religion doesn't directly impact many of our interactions, whether at work or in social settings, the beliefs of others shape their worldview and could inform many decisions that they make. A harsh reaction to something a colleague says or does may offend them because they spoke or acted based on a deep belief or conviction.

Large corporations such as Oil and Gas companies typically attract employees from a wide variety of backgrounds.

When we find ourselves working in large, multinational companies, we should not be surprised to encounter people who look different to us, and we should be sure to remove stereotypes and assumptions from our interactions.

Trevor was taken by surprise when the fully covered Muslim woman he had just met was introduced as the head of innovation of a large organization. He assumed that, because of her religious choices, she would align to a particular stereotype, a stereotype he was not even aware that he had. Fatema quickly proved all his biases wrong, from her strong, confident walk and North American accent to her dynamic, energetic, and articulate personality. Throughout their time working together, Trevor saw how incorrect the biases created by the "outer wrapping" were, and how biases such as his had contributed to Fatema's feeling that she had to compensate for the way she looked on the outside.

Getting the Conversation Started
Growing up

1. What is or are the important religions in your community?
2. How were different religions viewed and treated?
3. Was there a religious or spiritual background to your childhood, what impact did that have on you?
4. How is religion taught in your culture?
5. Is learning about (and teaching) religion mandatory in your culture? What happens to those who do not study as required?

Identity

6. How important is faith or religion? Why do you say so?
7. Is religion or faith the most important thing in your life? Why or why not?

8. What would be the consequence of someone pursuing their religion whole-heartedly?
9. Are faith and religion things that should be expressed outwardly, or kept private? How do you respond to private and public displays of religious beliefs?
10. What role does faith or religion play in your daily life: work, family, friendships, and society?
11. Describe how religion could be a core part of one's identity.
12. How does religion influence our culture and society?
13. Describe how religious differences played a role in a current or recent historical conflict.

Many of the conflicts we experience regarding religion are because of assumptions we make about things we don't know or understand. Rather than leading with our opinions about other faiths, consider instead listening to others share about their faith and then simply sharing our own. So, as a culturally agile learner, next time you're wanting to broach this subject, lead with questions. Perhaps, listen more than you speak, and you'll see a refreshing difference in how conversations turn out.

Digging Deeper
Diversity in Religion

14. Is your culture respectful of all faiths?
15. In your view, did God create cultural diversity? How do you believe that He feels about it?
16. How well do people of different faiths and religions interact with each other in your culture?
17. Explain why it is acceptable (or unacceptable) to worship God in many languages.

18. Describe the religious diversity in your home country. What makes it acceptable (or unacceptable) for people in your home country to have a faith different to yours?
19. What are the limitations around speaking about religion in your culture?
20. Can you convert to a different religion in your culture? If someone changes his/her religion, what would be the consequence?
21. In what ways does your religion allow (or not allow) others to practice different faiths?

Religion in the Workplace

22. How important is faith and religion in relating to colleagues or team members?
23. How much does the faith of your colleagues impact your interactions with them?
24. How has having the same (or different) religions contributed to the atmosphere in the work environment?
25. How does your company handle the different religious holidays on the calendar?

Inter-Religious Conversations

26. How can we respect each other regardless of our differences in beliefs and religion?
27. In what ways are religious conflicts leveraged by people in powerful positions to pursue their agenda/objectives?
28. How would you attempt to reverse misconception about your religion in the culture?
29. Do all religions share core values or are there key differences between them? Why do you believe that?

RELIGIOUS ACTIVITIES AND RITUALS

How do you express your faith and beliefs?

Discussing religion can indeed be challenging due to its deeply personal nature and the diversity of beliefs within any faith. Even within the same faith and religion, the experience and expression of that faith can differ from person to person because of the variety of denominations, sects, and faith communities that exist. In addition to these factors, our differences in personality and unique cultural journeys can make it feel like religion is a subject that is impossible to broach without somehow offending others. So, what do we do when we find ourselves at odds with people who share our beliefs?

A Christian small group was meeting online during the COVID-19 pandemic. A worksheet was sent out each week for members to complete as they listened to the Sunday sermon, and then the group met online during the week to discuss the previous Sunday's teaching. Their meetings seemed to be going well in general, but the facilitator noticed that a member of the group was becoming increasingly agitated as the weeks progressed. Each week, people would freely share their thoughts about Sunday's sermon and discuss what they had learned. Although openness and honesty were encouraged, one young woman was frustrated because she had systematically answered each discussion question on the weekly worksheet, but the group seldom discussed all the questions. She also felt that her limited knowledge of the Bible didn't allow her to participate freely in the "off script" discussions.

The Small Group Facilitator set aside time to speak to her one-on-one instead of challenging her agitation in front of the whole group. He communicated to her that there were no wrong answers, that each person was merely sharing their perspective about each answer. While he encouraged her to feel free to share her thoughts, he also addressed the matter of not sticking to the questions, expressing that the questions were a guideline meant to induce deeper discussion. In this way, he assuaged her frustration and helped her manage her expectations.

Getting the Conversation Started
Personal Religious Activities

1. How often, if ever, do you pray or commune with a higher power? Are there specific times or rituals mandated by your religious tradition?
2. Do you view religious activities as superficial cultural practices, or do they hold real and significant meaning to you? What informs your perspective on this matter?
3. What are benefits you derive from participating in religious traditions and activities? How do they contribute to your overall well-being and sense of fulfillment?

4. To what extent does religion influence your life choices and decision-making?
5. Which religious tradition holds the most significance for you? How does this tradition contribute to your spiritual journey and sense of identity?

Religious Activities and Society

6. What is your perspective on integrating religious activities into societal institutions or public life?
7. Are there any religious practices which have disappeared in your lifetime? What may have led to their decline or total disappearance?
8. Which religious festivals or rituals are recognized as national holidays in your country? What led to this integration?
9. Do you see value in embracing a diversity of religions, or do you believe the world would be better off if everyone followed the same faith? What informs your viewpoint on this matter?
10. Is religion a personal choice or communal identity? Should children be taught their parents' religion or given freedom to explore their own spiritual path?
11. Regarding prayer practices in your religion, are prayers typically offered privately, within the family or group setting, or exclusively within places of worship? Is there a requirement for prayers to be led by ordained religious figures?
12. At what point does a child become an adult in the eyes of your community or culture? How is this transition typically marked or celebrated?
13. Is there a specific religious celebration or ritual associated with the transition to adulthood in your culture or faith tradition? If so, can you describe it?

14. How do you think your family and community would react if you decided to change your religious affiliation or identity? What challenges or support might you anticipate in such a scenario?

15. Are there any religious activities or practices mandatory for individuals to join a religious group or community? What about maintaining a good standing within the group?

16. If you could only pass on one religious practice to your children, which would you choose and why? What significance does this practice hold for you personally, and why do you believe it is important to impart it to the next generation?

As we reconcile the differences that exist between even those who share the same faith, our global world pulls us ever closer to people who have completely different beliefs from us, people with whom it will be difficult to find religious common ground.

Enrique and Charlotte woke up one morning to a thumping noise. When they investigated the source of the sound, they found it was coming from their neighbor's backyard. A large group of people had gathered outside—to the couple's great surprise—to slaughter a cow. When Enrique and Charlotte had become spectators, the process was already quite far along and pieces of meat were neatly set aside. This was an unusual sight for the couple, who had never seen anything like it. After researching possible reasons for the killing of an animal in this way, they discovered their neighbors were following the sacred Muslim traditions of Eid al-Adha. Later that day, their neighbors brought them a generous three kilograms of meat, beginning a beautiful friendship.

Digging Deeper
The Religious Activities of Others

17. How do you believe individuals should demonstrate respect for the religious activities and practices of others?
18. Is it acceptable for individuals outside of your religious community to participate in your religious activities and rituals? What factors influence this decision, and what are your thoughts on inclusivity in religious practices?
19. In your workplace, do people celebrate inter-cultural holidays and religious observances together, or do they tend to keep such celebrations within their respective cultural or religious groups?
20. From your perspective, how challenging is it for individuals who do not belong to mainstream religious groups to achieve success and integration in society? What barriers or opportunities might they encounter along their journey?

Religious Perceptions

21. How do religious rituals shape cultural norms, values, and community interactions?
22. Reflecting on your upbringing, were there any religious traditions or activities that your family practiced, and how did they influence your understanding of faith and spirituality? What significance did these traditions hold for you personally?
23. How are atheists perceived and treated in your culture? Are there any common stereotypes or misconceptions associated with atheism?
24. Is religious practice considered a private matter in your culture? If so, what are some examples of acceptable private worship practices? How do individuals navigate the balance between personal faith and public expression of religious beliefs?

Religion, Friendships, and Relationships

25. Do you have friends who belong to different religious groups? If so, what factors influence your friendships across religious lines? If not, what are some reasons for this?

26. To what extent is it socially acceptable to form friendships with individuals from different religious backgrounds? Are there any societal norms or expectations regarding interfaith friendships?

27. How does your society view romantic relationships between people of different religions? Are there any challenges or barriers faced by couples with differing religious beliefs?

28. What role did religious activities play in your family growing up? Were they central or more peripheral?

29. Upon leaving your family environment, did you continue to engage in religious activities? What factors influenced your decision to maintain or discontinue these practices?

30. What motivates you to participate in religious activities? Do you view them as a duty, obligation, necessity, source of enjoyment, or as a means of fostering community connections?

RELIGIOUS LEADERS

Who should lead your religious community?

Religious leaders shoulder a significant responsibility in the eyes of their followers. Whether a leader chooses to shroud their role in mystery or remains transparent and accountable, it is hard to deny the significance of that religious leader's role in the lives of the people who follow them.

A local church in Nicaragua faced the challenge of electing leadership when they decided to add a new pastor to their eldership team. With the church experiencing growth, there was a need for elders who could effectively represent the demographic they served. Carlos emerged as a prime candidate for the role as he showed exemplary Christian character, a firm knowledge of Biblical teachings, and he was able to relate well with the people he would ultimately pastor. However, some elders harbored concerns about Carlos's theological convictions, as he appeared uncertain when responding to certain questions. To the elders, this made him seem suspicious and less suitable for the role.

During deliberations, one elder raised a point that hadn't been considered before that shed light on the situation. It was revealed that Carlos had tailored his responses to the Nicaraguan audience he would be serving. What the elders perceived as indecisiveness and suspicion in his tone was, in fact, an indirect communication style that Carlos intended to employ when ministering to his congregation. This was the very thing the eldership team needed: a means to communicate and connect with their Nicaraguan members.

Getting the Conversation Started
Religious Leaders in Society

1. How are religious leaders regarded in your community?
2. In what ways do religious leaders influence and shape your community?
3. To what extent do religious leaders influence societal issues and political matters?
4. What qualities differentiate religious leaders from leaders in business or politics?
5. In your opinion, what should be the extent of the connection between religion and politics, and why?
6. How significant is faith and belief in God or higher spiritual powers in society and leadership?

Perceptions of Religious Leaders

7. How do religious leaders specifically make your community either better or worse?
8. How are religious leaders perceived in comparison to other leaders in your culture?
9. Are religious leaders generally respected, or are they viewed with skepticism and carefully managed?

10. What are the primary reasons why individuals may hold negative opinions of religious leaders?
11. Conversely, what are the main reasons why people tend to view religious leaders positively?
12. In terms of overall trust in leaders within your community, how do religious leaders compare to other types of leaders?

"In our diverse international context, it's imperative to invest in unique IA competencies that will give us the tools to navigate ministry, build authentic community and model behaviors that are consistent with our beliefs as international churches. One of the greatest ways IA training will help us is by increasing our sensitivity to things we don't know or see as it relates to our context."

—Larry Henderson

Along with the responsibility of caring for members, religious leaders may find that they need flexibility in various aspects and dimensions of culture.

Elijah's experience as one of the elders in his religious community was not as seamless as he had anticipated. His early days were marked with tension and conflict because of his leadership style and some unmet expectations. Elijah had understood that he would have a more senior role in the leadership of the community and struggled to reconcile himself to the fact that he wasn't.

Another aspect that added to the strained atmosphere was a difference in worldview. Elijah primarily operated from an Innocence/Guilt worldview, relying on rules to resolve disputes, which clashed with the Power/Fear worldview of his fellow elders. To the leadership of the religious community, Elijah simply came across as an elder who didn't know his place, and sadly, he was let go from position.

Had Elijah grasped the dynamics of power within the community and honed his ability to communicate effectively—

both directly and indirectly—he might have been able to garner favor with followers and better serve the community.

Digging Deeper
Authority of Religious Leaders

13. What sort of power do religious leaders hold over their followers?
14. What is the role of religious leaders in people's day to day lives?
15. What are the significant life events or milestones in which religious leaders play a crucial role in your community?
16. To what extent is your religious leader important to you, or how much authority do they have in your life?
17. In your community, who holds authority on spiritual matters, and how did they gain that authority?

Religious Counsel and Correction

18. To what extent do you trust your religious leader for guidance and advice?
19. Do you believe all leaders should possess spiritual awareness or adhere to a specific religious doctrine?
20. In your religion, what are the procedures or criteria for excommunication or severing ties with individuals?
21. Can you share an experience where you have either encountered pain or found healing through the actions of a religious leader?
22. To what extent is it acceptable for religious leaders to publicly shame people?
23. What are the consequences for those who question religious leaders in your community?
24. Is it necessary to seek approval from a religious leader for significant life decisions?

25. Do you see religious leaders' role as enforcing traditional rules or interpreting them in modern life?
26. How do you cope with the adverse effects that certain religious leaders may have on your well-being or beliefs?

SACRIFICE

What is worth giving up something up for?

Have you ever left your place in a line and returned, expecting to rejoin the queue at the back, just to be waved right back into your original spot by the people who had been standing behind you? Or watched as someone ran into a burning building, and later climbed out of a second story window with a child in their arms? Or looked on as the crossing guard waved down a car that was driving too fast while they guided young children across a busy intersection?

Humans make sacrifices for one another every day; some are intense acts of life-saving bravery, and others are small moments that go unseen and unnoticed. Nonetheless, when a sacrifice is made for you, it is hard not to feel loved and cared for, even when it is the sacrifice of a stranger.

Nick and Katie experienced the gentle sacrifice of a stranger while they were traveling in Istanbul, Turkey. They had been in the country for a few days and had lost track of the date—forgetting that it was December 31st.

They walked through the streets near the Hagia Sophia in terrible weather, but wanted to make the best use of their time, taking in all that they could of this beautiful city. Nick and Katie stopped for a coffee and found themselves standing under an awning at a nearby restaurant chatting with a man lingering near the door. They spoke for a while and learned that the man was preparing his restaurant for a big New Year's Eve crowd. The smells coming from the kitchen were delightful, and the couple complimented him, asking if he was still receiving reservations for the evening. His reply was that he was no longer taking reservations, but to come after 9 p.m. and see him. He adamantly declared he would get them a seat!

The couple returned to their hotel to warm up and dry off. As the evening turned to night, they became tired, not wanting to make the long walk back to the restaurant, braving yet again the cold and rain. Part of their hesitancy to return was their lack of a reservation. Was it worth it to trust the words of the owner and risk being turned away after making the trip back out there? Katie had also forgotten the name of the restaurant owner, making her embarrassed to return. However, after a bit more deliberation, the couple decided to go.

As they neared the restaurant, the music was loud, the place was packed out, and Nick and Katie were disheartened. Just before turning around, Katie got up the courage to talk to the doorman and attempt to explain the conversation she had earlier that afternoon. She could tell that he, understandably, didn't believe her story. With the language barrier and her inability to give him the name of the person she had spoken to, Katie could tell she wasn't very believable. She asked to at least leave a note for the hospitable man, thanking him for his invitation and asking forgiveness for her rudeness. As she was finishing her note, a person put their hand on her shoulder. She turned around to see none other than the restaurant owner smiling at her, and the two joyfully began to greet. Before they continued speaking, Katie confessed to him that she did not know his name, and to her relief, he told her he felt the same because he had never given his name. They both laughed, and several other people joined their lively conversation. The man revealed his name to be Mustafa—and he told Nick and Katie that if they would wait about five minutes, their table would be ready. During their short wait, they chatted with some Turkish people outside who had heard the story. Their insight captivated Nick and Katie; the Turkish were surprised that the Americans would confess not knowing the owner's name and still want to honor him by showing up. They believed most Americans would not come if they did not have a reservation nor would a Westerner honor the owner's invitation in this bad weather.

The couple was soon escorted inside, and they noticed other guests watching—special care had been taken to prepare a place for them, and people noticed. Nick and Katie were honored and humbled that Mustafa would prioritize them in such a way even though they had just met. Their evening had undoubtedly been a time they would cherish deeply and never forget.

It is the people we meet that make our experiences things to remember. Going to a new place and seeing something beautiful is special, but it is only when you meet the people that give the place life that you cherish it. Even more so, when you experience sacrificial kindness, a moment turns into a memory.

Nick and Katie's decision to sacrifice their comfort led to a beautiful evening. Mustafa sacrificed space in his restaurant for his new guests, excited to seat them in a place of honor. On this particular night, the sacrifices seemed small, but their implications were great, mending false understandings and bridging cultural gaps.

Getting the Conversation Started

1. What does the word "sacrifice" mean to you?
2. What makes something a sacrifice?
3. Has anyone ever made a sacrifice for you? If so, why do you think they did it?
4. Have you ever sacrificed anything for someone else? Why did you do it?
5. What is the most significant example of sacrifice you have witnessed? Why was it significant to you?
6. How do you determine when a sacrifice is necessary?
7. How do you choose when to make a sacrifice?
8. Can someone sacrifice too much, or inappropriately? What is an example of where you have seen this?
9. Why are people who have made great sacrifices in history revered?
10. To what extent is it considered selfish to prioritize one's own needs over those of friends and family?
11. If someone makes a sacrifice for you, do you believe you are obligated to return the favor?
12. Are there differences in how different generations see sacrifice? How has this perception shifted over the last three generations?
13. What impact does sacrifice have on the recipient, and what do you believe is the appropriate response to it?
14. Do you think there are different societal expectations regarding sacrifice based on gender? If so, what are they?

Morality

15. Under what circumstances do you believe it's morally right to sacrifice for others?
16. Do you believe there's a limit to how far one should go when sacrificing for someone else?

17. Is there a limit to how much you would sacrifice for your family?
18. Do you consider it a sacrifice if fulfilling a duty or obligation?
19. Do you think true altruism is possible, and if so, how do you achieve it?
20. Should individuals relinquish their rights for the betterment of their community
21. Is there ever a situation where someone should be compelled or obligated to sacrifice their rights?
22. How would you distinguish between sacrifice and selfishness?
23. When do you think it's appropriate to sacrifice for others without expecting anything in return?
24. Have you ever felt pressured to sacrifice something for your community? What decision did you ultimately make, and why?
25. What are the implications of presuming someone's motives behind their act of sacrifice?

What would a parent do for their child? What would your parents do for you? The love of a mother and father has depth that cannot be described in words and limits that cannot be found. A parent's pursuit of the well-being of their child can sometimes mean the sacrifice of their own well-being.

Kwan and Ji-An's story exemplifies the profound sacrifices parents make for their children. Despite working in middle-management positions, they chose to invest significantly in their children's education, opting for private schooling and tutoring. This decision required not only a financial sacrifice but also humility.

Due to their investment in education, Kwan and Ji-An had to settle for more modest housing compared to their colleagues. They even shared a room as an office and often found themselves in simultaneous video conferences. To maintain appearances, they would frequently keep their cameras turned off, concealing their less-than-ideal working conditions. Unfortunately, this led some colleagues to misunderstand their situation and become frustrated with their apparent lack of engagement during calls.

However, beyond the financial sacrifice, Kwan and Ji-An demonstrated a willingness to forgo societal expectations and risk their social reputation at work. Their commitment to prioritizing family above all else is truly admirable and serves as a testament to the depth of parental love and sacrifice.

Digging Deeper
Personal

26. What does sacrifice in marriage entail, and how does it manifest in real-life scenarios?
27. Do you feel a sense of sacrificial obligation in your life? If so, in what aspects and to whom?
28. Reflecting on your priorities, what is the most significant aspect of your life, and what would you be willing to sacrifice for it?
29. Is sacrifice inherently beautiful? Why or why not, and what are the factors that influence its beauty?
30. In your opinion, what takes precedence: sacrificing personal desires for the sake of family, or sacrificing family ideals for personal desires? Explain your reasoning.
31. What obligations, if any, do children have toward their parents as a result of their parents' sacrifices? How can these obligations be expressed?
32. To what extent do cultural norms and personal values influence one's duty to sacrifice, and how does this duty vary in different contexts?

33. Can you recall instances in which you chose not to sacrifice something? What factors influenced your decision-making process?
34. How have stories of sacrifice, whether from religious texts, history, or personal experiences, impacted your understanding of sacrifice and its significance?
35. What is the most important thing in your life and what would you give up for it?
36. Do you consider sacrifice a beautiful thing? Why or why not?
37. What is more important—to sacrifice your own desires for the sake of your family? Or to sacrifice your family's ideals for the sake of your own desires? Why or why not?
38. What should you sacrifice for your parents? Do you owe them anything because of their sacrifice for you?
39. How far does your duty to sacrifice extend? and is there a right order for who it belongs to first?
40. Have you ever deliberately chosen not to sacrifice something? What led you to that decision?
41. Can you recall stories that you grew up with that exemplify sacrifice?

Sacrifice in Religion

42. If you are religious, how does sacrifice play a role in what you believe?
43. How does religion influence the perception of sacrifice within your community?
44. In what contexts is sacrifice considered an expectation within your religious tradition, and what are the underlying reasons for this expectation?
45. Who holds the authority to determine whether a sacrifice is appropriate within your religious framework, and what factors contribute to this determination?

RITUALS AND RITES OF PASSAGE

How do we mark change?

Exploring cultural rituals and rites of passage can be a fascinating intercultural conversation. According to the Merriam-Webster Dictionary, a rite of passage is a ritual, event, or experience that marks or constitutes a major milestone or change in a person's life. Conversation around events that shape a person's life journey will deepen our connection with them and help us reflect on the events that have shaped our own lives. One ritual common among many cultures worldwide is the milestone of marriage.

Marriage ceremonies are exercised in most of the world, but look different depending on where they are practiced. People from many cultures get married every day—often surrounded by family and close friends. Some tie long-standing family knots and others commit their life to someone they met in a pub a few hours prior. Some say "I do" in a lavish hotel ballroom, others while barefoot by the sea, and still others in a quiet courtroom.

For Rebecca, marriage was a rite of passage and a signifier of moving on to the next stage of life. Maturing, becoming a woman, growing into oneself and your purpose. She had attended many weddings because her husband was often asked to officiate them, and she always found it interesting being a bystander in this intimate moment of a stranger's life. Rebecca would notice the intense familial moments, secretive glances, and many other things in between. At one of these weddings, she found the ceremonial bouquet and garter toss to be livelier and more interactive than is typical. At weddings in the United States, it is common practice for the bride to throw her bouquet to the young single women and the groom to throw his wife's garter to the young single male guests. Whoever catches each lucky item is destined to be the next one married. This group, Rebecca noticed, had an interesting dynamic. The women were all incredibly eager to catch the bride's bouquet, vying for a spot close to the front and grappling for the bouquet once it was in the air. The men, on the other hand, were reluctant, stepping as far back as the dance floor would allow, and watching the garter land on the floor. It seemed none of them were ready to get married themselves!

Getting the Conversation Started
Becoming an adult

1. At what age does a child become an adult?
2. Is there a ceremony or celebration? Who is meant to attend? What is preparation like?
3. Did you have a coming-of-age ceremony?
4. Is this a practice you will maintain for your own family?

5. How do young people demonstrate they are "becoming adults"?
6. At what age are you considered a respectable member of the community?
7. Do teenagers have to complete a rite of passage to be considered adults?
8. Are there certain rituals and rites of passage connected to being part of a club or society (sports, scouts, orchestra, etc.)?

Marriage

9. How does the family or community prepare boys for marriage?
10. How does the family or community prepare girls for marriage?
11. How is marriage perceived in your culture to change an adult's life?

Familial expectations

12. Is there anything that your grandparents expected their grandchildren to do as a rite of passage? Did your parents go along with this desire out of respect, even if they did not support it?
13. Do you expect your children to carry on your family heritage through practicing the same rituals and rites of passage that you did with them? How will it affect your relationship should they choose not to?

Some of the ways culture is maintained generation to generation is through small gestures; they often go unnoticed but make the deepest relational impact. Scarlett's father continued a tradition that his own father had begun with him when he was starting a new phase of life as a young man. To be affirmed in your gifts and talents is powerful, especially when those affirmations come from those whom you love and revere. When Scarlett finished high school and traveled to study in another country, her father gifted her a letter, one that she continues to read to this day, because it speaks positive truth into her life and lifts her up from day-to-day challenges. The letter she received was not written a few minutes before she boarded her flight as a quick goodbye, but rather was carefully crafted, and powerfully delivered, and included several profound encouragements. The letter was affirming and called out the gift and talents that Rebecca's father saw in her.

Some rituals practiced today are the result of hundreds of years of tradition; others are new to a family or culture but are destined to have incredible impact down the line. Either way, rituals and rites of passage are wonderful topics to discuss in intercultural conversations.

Digging Deeper
Your Experience of Rites of Passage

14. Is there a particular age or experience that is considered a "milestone" in your adult life?
15. Do you think your culture's rites of passage impacted who you are today?
16. How would you be different had you not performed your family's cultural or religious rituals?
17. What was the most significant moment for you on your journey to adulthood?
18. When did you first become aware that there were certain rituals or rites of passage that were expected of you or of others in your culture?

Origins of rituals and rites

19. What are the origins of your familial or cultural rites of passage?
20. Why are your culture's rituals and rites of passage important and what purpose do they serve?
21. Are there old rituals that your ancestors used to practice which you know have been lost?
22. What rituals and rites of passage are religious in your family or community? Which are cultural?

Birthdays

23. Are there any special rituals or practices with new-born infants?
24. What birthdays are especially significant in a child's life? Why?
25. Do you celebrate other passings of time besides birthdays?
26. When is someone considered an elder in your community?

Death and grieving

27. Are there any rituals or practices to remember and honor people who have died?
28. Are there any rituals associated with the process of grieving in your culture?
29. Is death considered a rite of passage in your culture?
30. What are rituals and practices associated with the body after death?
31. Is there a specific place in which rituals surrounding the death of a loved one are performed?

GENERATIONAL RELATIONSHIPS

How do generations relate to each other?

With family, nothing is simple. With years of expectations and high emotion, with generational heritage to pass down, and desire to create one's own way, there's always more when it comes to family.

And Mariam's was no exception. Her family is from Jordan, where they had lived among the same tribe and in the same area for generations. Their family had established quite a name and heritage among the people with whom they lived. Mariam and her brother were set to inherit neighboring plots of land from their father but had different intentions on what they planned to do with it. Mariam had a desire to live an urban life, she wanted the funds to be able to start life in the city. She had offers of substantial amounts from people wanting to buy her land; however, they were strangers to the family. When it became known to the family that Mariam was considering selling her plot of land, especially to strangers, a conflict ensued.

Her land has been given to her as an honored gift, something to be cherished. It had depth of meaning for her family, part of a passing down of her family's generational roles. Eventually, she would have a family of her own with which to enjoy the land.

There are many facets to culture, it is complex and dynamic. Among cultures that are held accountable by the community, one of the complexities is the expectation to comply with the dominant wish of the community, which isn't something that can easily be negotiated with. For Mariam to even consider selling her family's heritage was an offense. So what is the right course of action for Mariam? Does she put her own desires aside in the name of honoring her heritage? Does she pursue the life that better fits her dreams for the future? Is there even a right course of action?

The answer is neither black and white nor linear. Oftentimes, you steer the ship in a certain direction, and if you have made your way into a storm, you have to endure, look for land, and trust that you will come out on the other side having learned a lesson, better equipped to handle the next storm, or better yet, steer away from it.

Mariam entered a storm when she began considering deviating from the dominant wish of her family. How she chose to move forward, who she spoke to and when, were key factors in determining how quickly she could steer away from the conflict.

Mariam found that, while of course her family wanted her to remain near to them and value the same things they did, they were pierced not from her wishes for a different life but rather her seeming lack of consideration for the situation she would be creating and leaving behind. They had no idea what the new landowners would be like or if they would align with the community. If she sold her land to strangers, her brother and his family could be in a difficult spot, having to cater to neighbors that they may not align with. In a society so oriented toward family, it is odd to have strangers so close to your life that are not a part of your community.

Mariam's brother had offered to buy her plot, but at a price much lower than the outside buyers were willing to pay. She continued to deliberate, not wanting to lose out on a beneficial financial situation, "supply and demand" as she called it. Her mother called her selfish, it was shameful to let a stranger have a piece of family land. "What will people say?", her brother lamented.

Ultimately, Mariam learned the proper decision would have been to sell the land to her brother, guaranteeing the inheritance remain in the family, honoring the community, while also preserving her opportunity to seek after that which she felt passionate about. By asking questions and finding out her family's opinions on her desire to sell her land, Mariam could have escaped the conflict within her family.

Getting The Conversation Started
Growing up

1. How does age dictate roles in the society where you grew up?
2. On whom does the responsibility of child rearing fall and why?
3. What age is the expected age for marriage and why?
4. What age is the expected age for a woman to have her first child? Why is that?
5. In what ways do very young children participate in family gatherings?
6. How are school-age children expected to behave at family gatherings?
7. What is the role of adolescents in the home?

Relatives

8. In what ways are children expected to have relationships with their cousins and aunts and uncles?
9. Are you expected to live near or with your parents as you get older and begin working? Why or why not?
10. In your culture, do multiple generations live in the same house? How do you feel about that?
11. In what ways is your greeting to the elderly in your community different from how you would address younger members of society?

Respect

12. Do you stand when someone older than you enters a room? Why or why not?
13. When there is an intergenerational meal, is a particular person or persons designated to partake of the food first? Why is that?
14. What do intergenerational meals look like, can everyone eat together or are certain age groups separated? If groups sit at different tables or places, who goes where, and which age groups sit together?
15. Is it customary to offer your seat to someone if they are older than you? Why or why not?
16. What is the expected age for retirement? Why is that the age?
17. What does a retired person do with their time?
18. Describe how age relates to power or sway within society.
19. Describe how younger generations view those who are older?

Generational relationships pan out differently around the globe. When a certain role is placed on someone because of their age, we expect that to never change. But as time goes on, roles need to change along with our capabilities. The Wang family experienced this firsthand with a Thanksgiving miscommunication.

Jie was becoming aware of the years taking a toll on her body. She was slowing down but had no desire to stop creating a space in her home for her family to gather, grandkids and all. The Wang's were Chinese American and a popular American holiday, called Thanksgiving, was coming around again. Jie had invited her children and their families to come over for the celebration, as well as a couple of women from their church community who had celebrated Thanksgiving with the Wang's for years (who they called "aunties"). While Jie historically took care of the main dishes and guests provided sides, Sophia, Jie's daughter, knew she needed to step in and take some of the hosting responsibilities off her aging mother. She created a spreadsheet to share with her mother and siblings so that it was clearly delegated what each person would be contributing to the meal.

The Wang's had a smooth family dynamic: they normally practiced clear communication and understood each other well. Jie and her husband came from China, but they raised all their children in the United States, so there were a few different worldview dynamics at play in their family. Jie held to a primarily Honor/Shame worldview, but her children ascribed to an Innocence/Guilt way of thinking due to their upbringing in the United States. Because of the varying worldviews at play, along with assumed generational roles, and the impact of honor and shame in the art of hospitality, an intercultural conflict ensued within the Wang family as Thanksgiving approached.

Two days before the big day, Sophia found out from her husband through the family grapevine that he, his wife, and children, had not been invited to the Wang's Thanksgiving, and that only his mother had been extended an invite. Sophia was in disbelief. She had grown up celebrating Thanksgiving with him and his mom, why should he not ·be invited now? Assuming there had been a mistake, Sophia messaged him letting him know that of course his family was invited to Thanksgiving, and they must join. Next, Sophia called her parents to ask about how this could have happened, but she was even more shocked by what she heard next. Her mother, Jie Wang, queen of an open and hospitable home, had chosen not to invite that man and his family. She admitted she was beginning to feel overwhelmed by having to host so many people and, in an attempt to employ a boundary, chose to keep the invite list smaller, something that does not come naturally to an Honor/Shame person. It was hard for Jie to do, but she felt like it was all she could handle.

Here, in the throes of conflicting cultural worldviews, intercultural agility and the ability to ask questions play powerful roles. Sophia can see that her mother is struggling due to her Honor/Shame worldview. Jie does not want to bring shame on anyone but is choosing to come to terms with her limited capabilities as she ages. Ascribing to an Innocence/Guilt frame of mind, all Sophia can see is that this man and his family had been wrongfully excluded, and this wrong needed to be righted.

Sophia was very honest and blunt in sharing how she felt about the situation. In her frustration, she verbalized to her parents how "rude" and "unkind" it was not to invite this family, and she unintentionally brought much shame upon her mother. In turn, Jie felt horrible about what happened and began considering ways to extend an invite to this family without being insulting. Situations like these can be diffused and even prevented, but it requires slowing down to take in all angles, observing from everyone's point of view. Had Sophia asked questions to better understand where her mother was at, she may have steered the family away from this storm.

In the end, the son and family of the aunty did end up with an invite from Jie and happily attended. The families enjoyed a beautiful Thanksgiving meal, without addressing the social faux pas that had occurred. While of course it's preferred to sidestep happenings like this one, they are always a learning experience and offer a great story afterward.

Digging Deeper
The Elderly

20. How formal were your interactions expected to be around your grandparents?
21. How are the elderly treated in your culture? Are they cared for by their families, or placed in an old age home?
22. Describe who offered wise counsel and gave support in your family, and how they did this.
23. How did your parents and grandparents relate to each other?
24. Was there a lot of interaction or engagement between multiple generations in your family or community and how do you think this shaped your worldview?

Looking to the future

25. Do you value living close to your parents and siblings? Why or why not?
26. How do grandparents, parents, and children display affection toward one another in your culture?
27. What does generational respect look like in a work environment?
28. How is leadership within your community transferred between generations?
29. How have you seen your role within your family and work life change as you have grown older?

KIDS AND UPBRINGING

How should children grow up?

Culture is a major aspect that shapes us as we grow up. In our formative years, we imitated our parents and caregivers as they lived with one of three worldviews: they pursued honor and avoided shame; they aligned with those in power instead of living in fear; or they ensured their innocence to avoid being found guilty. Without explicitly telling us, our parents taught us the worldview which formed our own view of the world. We, in turn, navigate the world with a certain perspective that we then pass on to those who come after us.

We don't really become aware of the impact of culture on our upbringing until we interact with others. Each friend we make opens our eyes to a different way of doing things, and a different view of various aspects of life. As we grow in our own culture and learn to relate with the cultures around us, we tend to make friends with people we have much in common with and avoid those from whom we vastly differ, evading the challenges that come along with that. At times, however, there are differences in culture and upbringing that we cannot avoid.

Priscilla, raised in a culture that values the privacy of personal life, was struggling to adjust to the relationship with her in-laws. Her husband was raised in a home where there was no regard for private, personal life. As such, Priscilla grew frustrated when her in-laws seemed to continually ask questions about her kids, job, and other parts of her personal life, even when her husband was not there. Although their curiosity was a cultural norm, Priscilla felt that it was an intrusion on parts of her life that she preferred to keep private. Being married to someone who'd had a completely different upbringing was causing tension, and Priscilla couldn't avoid the challenges that these differences were causing. As she grew in her intercultural agility, Priscilla was able to see the positive intentions behind her in-laws' actions. While it is still difficult at times, she has been able to adjust and feel calmer and less protective in conversation with them. She sees their curiosity as a sign of their love and even began to look forward to their visits as an opportunity to build on their relationship.

We are constantly learning more about ourselves and how we respond to others from a culture different from our own. If we're on this unique journey, then we can be assured that others are going on a similar journey of their own.

Getting the Conversation Started
Your Upbringing

1. What did your family value most growing up?
2. What was the most important thing your parents taught you growing up?
3. In which way is it significant to be the oldest or youngest born in the family?
4. What is interaction typically like between siblings?

5. What are common rites of passage for children in your community?
6. What are the stories that children are told? Rhymes? Myths/legends? Historical/cultural tales? Family lore?
7. To what extent is it necessary to have grandparents involved in children's lives in your community?
8. How are girls and boys perceived differently as they grow up?
9. What kinds of chores or responsibilities do children learn/have in the home and at what age do they start doing those things?
10. At what age should children start their formal education and why?
11. What age did you start your formal education? And why?
12. Why is culture important for kids to understand?
13. Is spanking children appropriate? When is it unacceptable/forbidden or appropriately viewed and used?
14. Why should children be disciplined? (Disrespect, disobedience, or defiance, etc.)
15. What types of discipline were used in your community to discipline children?
16. How have the types of discipline used in your community changed in recent years?
17. Are both girls and boys taught how to cook and clean? What is the reason for this?
18. Who is generally the primary caretaker/caregiver of the children in your family and community?
19. Growing up, were children shamed if they did something wrong?
20. Is it ok for the youngest girl in the family to marry first? Why or why not?

Traits we are born with and the habits we learn during our upbringing become inextricably connected by the time we are adults. It's hard to tell whether we are who we are because of our innate personality and talents, or because of the environment in which we grew up.

Maya was having a difficult time disciplining her son. At the time, the eight-year-old boy was displaying defiance and would react when he wasn't in control. Maya had just embarked on her journey of Intercultural Agility, and the perception management and self-reflection tools revealed that some of her son's behaviors were consistent with behaviors she had exhibited at that age. Digging deeper, she began to realize that, while her son shared her worldview, his expression of some aspects of culture were different because she was raising him away from their home country. The worldview she had grown-up in was being challenged, and she would need to be flexible in how she related to her son. Through understanding the differences between her unique culture and her son's, Maya was able to improve her relationship with her son and expand her views on how to raise him.

Something that Maya learned through this experience is that although we are raised with a certain worldview, other paradigms that we have been exposed to may influence the way we view the world and alter our expression of culture. It also means that those who come after us—our children, our nieces, and nephews, and those we care for and mentor— may also shift their worldview as they have their own unique cultural experiences. We have little to lose when we take a step back from our frustration and consider the upbringing and unique cultural journeys of those around us.

Digging Deeper
Raising kids

21. What roles do extended family members play in the upbringing of your child?

22. How important is it to have a strong connection with your in-laws for the sake of your children?
23. Who is the authority at home? The mother, father, both, or someone else?
24. At which age should kids first have sexual education? Why?
25. Is it common in your culture to have parents from two different cultural backgrounds?
26. With your role in the family, how do you model the important values and behaviors that you would like your kids to emulate and develop?
27. How did the way that you were raised communicate the spoken and unspoken values of your immediate family/family of origin?

Raising kids overseas [8]

28. If you are living in a different city or country than you were raised, how does raising children in a different culture enrich their upbringing?
29. Where have your kids grown up?
30. Which country do they feel is their home?
31. Which country is their favorite?
32. What are ways that children play in your culture—games? sports? toys?
33. Are there songs that children learn to sing?
34. How many children do families in your culture typically have? What is the gap between different siblings?
35. How are children seen in society and in families?
36. What was the most important thing your parents taught you growing up?
37. How have you seen your children influence positive change as a result of their exposure to a variety of cultures?

---

[8] A note for if someone does not have their kids living with them (which can be true for many expats): Ask who they live with and how often they visit, and praise the connection that videochats has in staying connected and give praise to the good care from the family member who is looking after them- it is significant in these situations. Never judge them for the great sacrifice they have made for their family.

38. What are some practical tips that you can offer to those raising their children abroad?
39. Where does the rest of your family live?
    a. How often do you get to visit them?
    b. Do they get to visit you?

ONE FINAL QUESTION

It is our hope that throughout this book of intercultural questions you have discovered that each person you encounter has a unique cultural wiring, a "self-culture." Although two people may share the same ethnicity, nationality, or passport country, their cultural journeys may be vastly different.

As our world becomes more globalized, we must find ways to break down the "single stories" that exist of other countries and cultures. Asking good questions is a crucial skill in becoming a cultural learner and building strong relational connections with people who are different than yourself. Good questions and good listening skills can help break down walls that hinder positive interactions between people of different cultural backgrounds.

You've used the questions in this book to unlock the cultural learner within. You picked up this book and used it to facilitate discussions because you were curious about culture.

So, what will you do now? How do you equip yourself with practical tools that deepen your intercultural agility and enrich your intercultural interactions?

Discover Your Own Self-culture

KnowledgeWorkx offers a range of tools designed to support you in maintaining the momentum you've gained from this book and furthering your intercultural journey. One such tool is the Three Colors of Worldview©, which provides insights into your cultural motivators and helps you understand what drives others. Utilizing this tool can be a powerful next step in enhancing intercultural agility within your communities and interactions.

Once you have an understanding of the foundational cultural motivators, the Culture Mapping Inventory will reveal your unique mix of the 12 Dimensions of Culture©. Armed with this understanding and equipped with neutral language, you'll be empowered to build bridges between individuals with diverse cultural backgrounds, fostering greater understanding and collaboration in your interactions.

Perception Management

The challenges we encounter in relationships are often rooted in our perceptions of ourselves, others, and our interactions within cultural contexts. These perceptions shape our emotions, thoughts, and actions, influencing how we interpret situations and make decisions. If left unchecked, our perceptions can lead to narrow-mindedness and critical interactions. However, we can become cultural learners, embracing diverse perspectives to foster dynamic and successful collaborations in organizational teams and community groups.

Engaging in perception management allows us to pause, identify biased thoughts, and expand our perspectives to respond meaningfully to others. By starting with self-awareness, we can develop strategies for effective communication and interaction. KnowledgeWorkx provides tools to recognize our own perceptions and behavioral tendencies, enabling us to leverage this awareness in our interactions with others. Through this process, we can cultivate understanding and synergy within diverse environments.

"As a professional in a multinational company, with offices around the world and approximately 17,000 staff in different countries and locations, I feel it is a basic need for me to have the knowledge and the tools in order to, first of all, be able to communicate and engage with people effectively from my side, but also to mentor and coach staff and leaders on how to do this, in order to create an inclusive, empathetic and efficient organization, regardless of nationality and location."

—Maria Manzoor

Cultural Learner and Intercultural Agility

These perception management tools empower individuals to embrace the role of cultural learners. A cultural learner is characterized by their curiosity and willingness to understand the motivations behind behaviors, including their own, rather than passing judgment on differences. They recognize that while individuals may belong to larger cultural groups, each person's journey is uniquely shaped by their own cultural experiences.

Remaining stagnant in one's perceptions and refusing to embrace cultural learning can lead to adopting a negative stance as a cultural critic. This mindset often involves believing that one's own culture and worldview are superior, thereby devaluing alternative perspectives. Such an attitude can strain relationships and hinder open communication, eroding trust and hindering group cohesion.

Conversely, as a cultural learner, one acknowledges the diversity of viewpoints in any given setting and seeks to broaden their worldview. This foster improved communication and problem-solving skills, leading to greater synergy within teams and groups. By embracing intercultural agility, individuals can positively influence their interactions and contribute to the success of their teams and organizations.

"We need IA to help us team multiculturally, authentically, where every member of the group has a voice and an equally weighted opinion. IA is a crucial tool for navigating communication gaps, negotiating contracts, understanding and rightly assessing unfamiliar target markets, entering those new markets as a multinational 'outsider' entity, and developing high-performing workers and teams."

—Joy Golson

High Performing Intercultural Team

Now, envision a scenario where every member of your team is transitioning from being a cultural critic to becoming a cultural learner. The Intercultural Agility framework, founded on perception management and self-cultural analysis, emerges as a potent tool for guiding individuals through discussions aimed at identifying enabling and disabling team behaviors. The insights generated by these tools can be harnessed to cultivate an interculturally agile group or workforce, fostering synergy and success. Teams and groups embarking on this journey toward intercultural agility can anticipate the following outcomes:

- **Fostering a Sense of Belonging**

By prioritizing behavior-based trust, the team cultivates an environment where every member feels a sense of belonging.

- **Enhancing Communication**

Overcoming barriers that impede communication leads to the establishment of healthy and effective channels for exchanging ideas and information.

- **Alignment Around Common Goals**

Establishing protocols for acknowledging and rectifying behavior helps the team align around a shared purpose, fostering unity and cohesion.

- **Building Relational Capital**

Meaningful relationships are forged within the team, resulting in the development of strong relational capital that bolsters collaboration and teamwork.

As the team collectively pursues intercultural agility, it creates a unique intercultural space where each member feels valued, understood, and accepted. Trust flourishes, and ideas flow freely, propelling the team toward achieving remarkable feats in our modern, globally interconnected world. With a unified front, little stands in the way of the team's collective success.

EPILOGUE

Your contribution to the next edition of this book

Your journey as a cultural learner doesn't have to end here. Whether you bought this book intentionally in your pursuit of becoming more culturally aware, or stumbled upon it unexpectedly, it's likely that it has left a lasting impact on your path as an intercultural learner.

As you continue your unique cultural journey, you may find yourself formulating questions of your own that deepen your interactions with others.

We believe that growth is most impactful when shared. We invite you to be a part of our collective growth by sharing any new questions you develop along the way at interculturalquestions.com/submit. Your insights may even find their way into the next edition of this book! The journey of a cultural learner is ongoing—let's continue growing together.

Submit Your Questions Here

ACKNOWLEDGMENTS

As I delved deeper into intercultural work, I met Bob Teeter, a gentleman who wrote many books about questions. He challenged me saying, "Marco, the world needs a book on intercultural questions. We need excellent questions to engage across cultures." I want to thank Bob for his challenge because it has resulted in this book.

I would also like to thank all the incredible Intercultural Agility Practitioners who contributed stories and questions to this book. It is an honor to bring together so much cultural understanding and wisdom.

ABOUT THE AUTHOR

Marco is a true international citizen. Originally from the Netherlands, his fascination with global work and culture has led him to work in over 70 countries. Realizing that international workers needed to be better equipped with intercultural intelligence led him to start KnowledgeWorkx in 2001.

As International Director of KnowledgeWorkx, Marco created the Inter-Cultural Intelligence (ICI) methodology for people development. In a world that needs more human connection, he is passionate about equipping people and organizations with the tools they need to enhance relational success with people around them.

Marco brings 28 years of intercultural work experience into everything he does – as a skilled facilitator and coach, he uses the KnowledgeWorkx ICI methodology to equip people with intercultural agility, giving them the best chance of not only succeeding, but thriving in our increasingly global world.

By volunteering for not-for-profit organizations, he assists with the development of intercultural agility for their organizations and people.

Marco lives with his family in the UAE. He is interculturally married and has the privilege of raising four 'Third Culture Kids'.

ABOUT KNOWLEDGEWORKX

The founders of KnowledgeWorkx started the company because they consistently found themselves doing cultural advising while consulting on strategic planning. One could not be separated from the other.

Thus, KnowledgeWorkx was launched with a vision to create a new framework for understanding problems and creating solutions. One that is accurate, integrated and innovative. Since its inception, KnowledgeWorkx products have evolved and been tested over 70 countries on five continents, and proven to be globally effective.

Over the last 20 years KnowledgeWorkx has continued to develop solutions that are global, locally relevant, holistic and practical. Its innovative approach delivers integrated and effective solutions using the Inter-Cultural Intelligence (ICI) framework and assessments in consulting, coaching, learning, and development.

Its solutions create a progressive and natural connect between national, personal, team and organizational culture. Because at its core, "Organizational culture is the sum total of the expression of the thinking, speaking and acting of its contributors."

You can learn more about the work KnowledgeWorkx does at: www.knowledgeworkx.com.

QUESTION INDEX

Achievement and Accomplishment

1. How is recognition shown in your culture?
2. Is recognition important in your culture? How is this demonstrated in your culture?
3. What is more appreciated in your community—status or accomplishment?
4. What would be considered "healthy" achievements?
5. Does greater achievement or accomplishment mean that you have a higher social standing?
6. What is considered a significant achievement in the community in which you grew up?
   a. How would that kind of achievement be rewarded?

7. When accomplishment is celebrated, does reward involve a physical object?
   a. What objects are common rewards?

8. Are any goals or pursuits passed down from one generation to another?
9. What are some examples of rewarding individual and group accomplishments?
10. Is it acceptable to show your neighbors and community how successful you are?

11. How far should people be willing to go to achieve their goals?
12. Are there any measures to achieve success that are frowned upon in your community?
13. How does society perceive people who haven't achieved much individually, but have contributed to or facilitated the success of others?
14. If you achieve success, are there certain things expected of you by people around you (colleagues, family, friends, etc.)?
15. Are there certain accomplishments that make you better suited for a future life partner?
16. Are certain pursuits higher in approval ranking than others and are these pursuits similar for both men and women?
17. How is the pursuit of achievement taught to children (at home, in school and in society)?
18. If you produce twice as much as any other colleague, how do you expect to be rewarded?
19. Would you hire someone with more steady experience, or someone with less experience and a short, impressive track record?
20. If your colleague gets a promotion because their sibling is the boss, is this acceptable to you?
21. How does your family celebrate your accomplishments?
22. How do you personally celebrate success or achievements?
23. Do your family's accomplishments influence the way you must live your life?
24. What personal or family accomplishment are you most proud of?
25. What behaviors do you adopt to show someone recognition?
26. In what ways are you encouraged to reward others?

27. What would you most like to accomplish and be recognized for? What do you hope your children will accomplish and be known for?
28. Do you value words and actions of appreciation for constant achievement?
29. What is your motivator to reach an accomplishment?
30. Are your goals primarily externally or internally motivated?
31. Is it acceptable to pursue your personal goals without taking your family's ideals into consideration?
32. What are examples of moral, ethical, and religious boundaries that need to be adhered to when you pursue your ambitions?

Conflict and Restoration

1. When you feel wronged, what is the first thing you do and why?
2. What could people say and/or do to repair wrongs and relationships?
3. What is the best way to express an apology?
4. If there is an issue, do you work to solve it, or do you ignore it?
5. Is conflict better handled directly or indirectly? Why do you say so?
6. Why is admitting wrong and apologizing important (or not important) in conflict resolution?
7. Has your view of the role and process of conflict and restoration evolved over time and if so, how?
8. How does your community view conflict?
9. What is a culturally appropriate way to express frustration with others?
10. How is restoration done if there is a conflict between two families? What about between two family members?
11. Should conflict be resolved in the open or kept private? Why?

12. Which types of conflicts should be handled in the open and which must be handled behind closed doors?
13. What behavior would you expect from a person who has an opposing view to yours?
    a. How does your family handle conflict?
    b. Does this reflect the social norms around you?
    c. What works well or does not work well with this?
14. How does your extended family solve conflicts?
15. How does your company handle conflict with employees or customers? Is it the same?
    a. Does this reflect the social norms?
    b. What works well or does not work well with this?

16. Which is easier to say: "I am sorry," or "I forgive you"? Why is that one easier for you to say than the other?
17. How do cultural differences cause conflict?
18. Would discussing cultural differences or cultural similarities bring people closer?
19. How can conflict best be avoided?
20. What does justice mean to you?
21. What impact does someone's power over you have in a conflict?
22. If there were a community court in your community, how would issues be dealt with?
23. Under what circumstances might it be appropriate for third-party mediators to help with conflict or resolution? What would that be like?
24. When an individual has a different opinion than a leader of a group, should they speak up in a group setting, or should they bring it up quietly behind-the-scenes? Does their status, age, or gender matter?
25. When there are issues of mistrust between conflicting parties (including family members), what practical steps could be taken to build trust, and bring healing or restoration?

26. What does forgiveness look like?
27. Some cultures say, "apology requested" and "apology accepted." What does that mean to you?
28. What is the best way to express an apology?
29. Can you separate the emotional from rational in issues? What is helpful or unhelpful about this ability in conflict?
30. Who is allowed to show anger and who is not? Why?
31. In which situations is it more or less appropriate to show anger or frustration?
32. Which emotions are appropriate to show in public?
33. In the culture you grew up in, what are some long-standing conflicts that haven't been resolved?
34. What for you is the most challenging conflict you've experienced. Were you able to overcome it and how?

Change

1. Is change good or bad or neutral? Why?
2. How do you react to change in general?
3. What's your view of change and how do you usually manage it when it occurs?
4. What framework do you use to decide whether a change is good or not?
5. If a change is bad, what redeems it or makes it a good thing to pursue?
6. What are the key ingredients necessary for bringing people with you through change successfully?
7. What does your weekly life look like? Do you have the same routines each week, or are your activities more varied? Why is that?
8. At what speed do you embrace adapting to change?
9. What aspects of life should never change?
10. How best can you handle an unfavorable change to your advantage?

11. Do you find that people overreact to change or underreact? Why do you say so?
12. How important is it for you to change?
13. What do you value more: continuity and stability, or change and creativity? Why?
14. What was the most difficult transition in your life, why do you think it was so hard?
15. What is the hardest part of change for you?
16. Is your society changing in the right or wrong ways? How so?
17. Who in your team is always open to change and who struggles to accept it?
18. How did your company handle the changes and challenges that occurred during Covid? Did you approve of these changes?
19. How do you view different countries' responses to the changes caused by Covid? How did that compare to your country?
20. In your childhood, did your parents change jobs often? How did that affect you?
21. How have activities around holidays and religious festivities changed over the years?
22. In some cultures, the "keeper of tradition" is seen as the most honorable person. Is that true of your culture, and how do they ensure tradition is maintained?
23. How would a dramatic job change be received by your family?
24. Is international travel encouraged in your family? Why or why not?
25. How would your family respond if you chose to live and work abroad?
26. How does your family show their approval (or disapproval) of a life change you make?
27. How did you and your family manage the changes that were brought about during Covid?

28. How does change affect culture?
29. To what extent is cultural change acceptable or a "good thing"? Why?
30. Does your culture treat change as a positive or negative thing? Why do you say so?
31. What could be considered barriers to cultural change?
32. In what ways does your culture and upbringing affect your ability to change?

Decision-making

1. Do you share your thoughts with other people when you make decisions, or do you prefer to make them alone? Why?
2. Are personal decisions made by the individual? Are family and friends involved in personal decision-making?
3. How does youth or age difference influence your perceived ability to make decisions?
4. How would you respond to someone who was unable to handle the consequences of their decision after they had ignored your advice?
5. Are there cultural traditions and protocols that impact decision making processes?
6. How do you make important decisions in your life? How was this shaped by the way that you saw others in your life make decisions?
7. Are there important decisions where the whole community gets involved and what process is followed to make that happen?
8. Are there decisions in life that are best made by people in authority over you (who to marry, what to study, where to live etc.)? Why?
9. Who is involved in group decisions in your family?

10. Who makes the major decisions in a typical family in your society (the father, the mother, an older sibling, a grandparent)?
11. How did your parents divide decision making responsibilities for your family?
12. Should personal decisions be made individually or in community? Why?
13. If a decision is made that shames the family, how is that communicated?
14. In a private family setting is disagreement permitted? How does that influence the way conversations are managed?
15. Describe a situation(s) where your personal preferences and the preferences of your family were not aligned.
16. How does gender influence how you can contribute to a decision-making conversation in your family?
17. How would you describe the process of when someone in your family begins making decisions on their own?
18. Who should be involved in group decisions at work and why?
19. Are there certain decisions or announcements that must be made face-to-face? How would you communicate to a staff member that he/she is fired?
20. If you are in a business meeting with a client with your boss, are there certain protocols that will dictate how/when you can contribute to the conversation?
21. How does a leader gather the information/opinions they need to make a decision?
22. If you have a different opinion from your team leader on a subject, is there a culturally appropriate way for you to communicate your viewpoint?
23. What does clear communication look like to you?
24. What is the importance of the communication method in decision making?
25. How do you talk about a decision before it is made? How do you communicate a decision after it is made?

26. How should confrontation be approached when you are angry with a decision?
27. In what ways are positive and negative emotions communicated and what communication channels are acceptable for either negative or positive emotions?
28. How does your supervisor/boss communicate decisions?
29. What style of communication does your supervisor/boss use according to their cultural background?
30. How does your boss's style of communication impact you?
31. Is your supervisor/boss more rational or emotional? How does that affect you?
32. Is your supervisor/boss more direct or indirect? How does that affect you?
33. How is being in public disagreement with someone else perceived in your culture?

Differences

1. In what ways do you intentionally differentiate yourself from your culture or community? And when is it important to do so?
2. Are there certain ages or circumstances in your culture where people normally differentiate themselves from others?
3. What differences do you appreciate most in other people?
4. What differences in others make you uncomfortable?
5. What are some distinct ways that members of your community are considered "different" and why do you think that is?
6. Describe how fashion trends in your country or community are similar or different to western fashion trends. What does it take for an outsider to become part of a group and belong in that group?
7. Who do you consider "different" from you and in what ways?

8. When you were growing up, did you feel like you were free to be yourself and were your unique differences valued? Why or why not?
9. How much appreciation of diversity is there in your friendship group or work team?
10. What does "celebrating differences" mean to you?
11. What makes someone an outsider in your social or work contexts?
12. If somebody is considered "not normal" in your community, how are they typically described?
13. Are there certain jobs that are not acceptable for certain groups or people in society?
14. Growing up, how were people with differing learning abilities treated in your school? Were they integrated or separated?
15. How are people with mental or physical disabilities included in society and the world of work?
16. If a person has a physical or mental disability, to what extent should they be part of public life?
17. In what ways do religious views impact how mental and physical handicaps are perceived?
18. Is accommodation offered for people who are physically or mentally handicapped in your culture? (sign language interpretation of live speeches, wheelchair access of public buildings and hotels/restaurants, etc.)
19. How accessible does the government of your country make communication for people who speak the minority language?
20. Discuss the factors that contribute to the positive, neutral, or negative vocabulary used to describe people with physical or mental disabilities in your community.
21. When does "being different" become a problem in the community?

22. How could someone differentiate themselves in your culture? What do you think of the idea that "Today's 'different' is tomorrow's normal'"?
23. Describe the cultural and racial diversity of your childhood friendship groups.
24. When, if ever, is it acceptable to date or marry someone of a different race or culture?
25. How are different sexual orientations perceived in your culture?
26. In what ways is the younger generation allowed to be different from the older one?
27. Discuss the factors that contribute to the positive, neutral, or negative vocabulary used to describe various sexual orientations in your community.

Education

1. Can you share with me about your learning journey?
2. What did you study at school, and do you find it prepared you for what came next?
3. What would you change about the way you were educated?
4. What was valued most in your school by students?
5. What was valued most by teachers?
6. Do you find higher education or skill training more practical or beneficial?
7. What is more valuable—formal or informal education?
8. What was the grading system like in your schools?
9. Did you find it to be equitable?
10. What do parents hope for when it comes to the educational pursuits of their children?
11. Do you find that students value receiving an education?
12. Is higher education after secondary school an expectation from parents?

13. What kind of extracurricular education might children engage in? Sports? Arts? Music? Other?
14. Is it acceptable to engage in free and open discussion and debate within the classroom or are students expected to absorb material from lecturer, without conversation?
15. What freedom do students have to question or disagree with their teachers?
16. In cultures that values formal education, how can or should the importance of informal education be raised?
17. What does the future look like for home schooling children or self-taught professionals?
18. How valuable is textbook learning? Do you see it offering more than life experiences?
19. Should creativity be encouraged in education?
20. To what extent should an emphasis be placed on rote learning and memorization?
21. To what extent should problem solving be taught in school?
22. What is discipline like in schools for children in your community? Are there punishments and rewards?
23. Are there schoolwide/city/state/national standards for testing or achievement?
24. What makes someone qualified to be a teacher?
25. Are teachers typically male or female?
26. What is the role of education in your society?
27. Is education necessary for a society? Why or why not?
28. What was your parents' connotation when they talked about education and what did that communicate to you about their worldview?
29. Is education equally necessary for both genders in your culture?
30. What is the expected level of education for boys and for girls?
31. What do you hope for the educational future of your own children?

32. What role does or should religion play in education?
33. What do you feel religious education is like?
34. Does your culture correlate level of education with status?
35. What are the social connotations between public and private education?
36. Is continuing education acceptable for adults?
37. In higher education settings, how important is hierarchy, especially between students and professors?
38. Is there military education or training in your community?
39. What is training like for tradespeople?
40. What does continuing education look like for tradespeople?
41. What education do you look for when you hire?
42. How are educators valued and well paid in society?
43. What level of status do teachers have?
44. In what ways is education seen as uniquely respected status?

Ethics and Morality

1. Why are ethics important in culture?
2. What are some ethical standards that you believe all cultures hold?
3. Do you have a strict moral code? Why do you hold to that?
4. Is morality culturally determined or individually determined? Why do you think so?
5. To what extent do "white lies" exist in your culture?
6. What is an example of when it is acceptable to tell a white lie?
7. When is it acceptable to break the law?
8. What's the difference between legality and morality? Which one is more important?
9. How do you teach your kids ethics?
10. How are ethics and morals taught by those around you?

11. Who is involved in the process of teaching ethics and morals?
12. What behaviors prove that you are ethical and which ones show you aren't?
13. Where do your ethics or morality come from? Where did you learn them originally?
14. What is the role of education in transferring ethics and morals?
15. Can your ethics or morality change over time? Have yours?
16. If they changed, where did you learn this new standard?
17. In which way does religion play a role in setting the standards and communicating ethics and morality?
18. Which leaders in society are perceived to have high morals and ethics and which leaders are perceived to have low ethics and morals?
19. How is win–lose negotiating viewed in society? Is striking a hard bargain at the expense of the other party applauded or frowned upon?
20. Have any moral and ethical values been undermined (in your community) in recent years and why has this happened?
21. What needs to happen to bring back some of the lost moral and ethical fabric in society?
22. How is receiving bribes and kickbacks perceived where you grew up? What are examples from different spheres of society where these practices might exist?
23. Are ethics classes taught in higher education and what would be examples of degree programs where this is happening?
24. Who are the parties or groups in society that you believe perpetuate immoral or unethical practices and which parties or groups are working together?
25. Has your experience in life been consistent with the system of ethics and morality you were taught growing up?

26. What is more important, doing what you have been taught is right, or doing what is legally correct?
27. When is it acceptable to choose family over doing what is right?
28. Is it more important to be right or honest or to protect the feelings of another person, even if it means bending the truth?
29. What are examples of the highest virtue in your culture?
30. Is it important to have a shared value system and/or set of beliefs when discussing matters of ethics and morality? If so, what is it, and how do you approach that?
31. How important are morals and ethics compared to achieving high grades in education and what are examples of way students (and their parents) are compromising on their morals to ensure high grades?
32. Is achieving success and being morality or ethics upright connected to each other? What are examples where they are and what are examples where they are not connected?

Faith and Religion

1. What is or are the important religions in your community?
2. How were different religions viewed and treated?
3. Was there a religious or spiritual background to your childhood, what impact did that have on you?
4. How is religion taught in your culture?
5. Is learning about (and teaching) religion mandatory in your culture? What happens to those who do not study as required?
6. How important is faith or religion? Why do you say so?
7. Is religion or faith the most important thing in your life? Why or why not?
8. What would be the consequence of someone pursuing their religion whole-heartedly?

9. Are faith and religion things that should be expressed outwardly, or kept private? How do you respond to private and public displays of religious beliefs?
10. What role does faith or religion play in your daily life: work, family, friendships, and society?
11. Describe how religion could be a core part of one's identity.
12. How does religion influence our culture and society?
13. Describe how religious differences played a role in a current or recent historical conflict.
14. Is your culture respectful of all faiths?
15. In your view, did God create cultural diversity? How do you believe that He feels about it?
16. How well do people of different faiths and religions interact with each other in your culture?
17. Explain why it is acceptable (or unacceptable) to worship God in many languages.
18. Describe the religious diversity in your home country. What makes it acceptable (or unacceptable) for people in your home country to have a faith different to yours?
19. What are the limitations around speaking about religion in your culture?
20. Can you convert to a different religion in your culture? If someone changes his/her religion, what would be the consequence?
21. In what ways does your religion allow (or not allow) others to practice different faiths?
22. How important is faith and religion in relating to colleagues or team members?
23. How much does the faith of your colleagues impact your interactions with them?
24. How has having the same (or different) religions contributed to the atmosphere in the work environment?
25. How does your company handle the different religious holidays on the calendar?

26. How can we respect each other regardless of our differences in beliefs and religion?
27. In what ways are religious conflicts leveraged by people in powerful positions to pursue their agenda/objectives?
28. How would you attempt to reverse misconception about your religion in the culture?
29. Do all religions share core values or are there key differences between them? Why do you believe that?

Friendship

1. Are your friendships based on common interests or with people you have context with?
2. What is the spark that creates a connection with someone who eventually becomes a friend?
3. Do you have a large group of friends, or do you prefer a smaller circle?
4. Do you have a childhood best friend?
5. Can friendships be developed freely or are there community rules that guide friendships?
6. What is the trait you look for in a friend above all others?
7. What happens first—building trust or building relationship? How do these two work together?
8. What is your favorite way to spend time with your friends?
9. How much time do you spend with friends?
10. How long does a friendship last?
11. If you are not in close physical contact with someone, what is the expectation for a friendship over a distance?
12. Do close personal friends become "part of the family"?
13. Would you consider your closest friendships to be with family or people outside of your family?
14. What does it mean to be a good friend?
15. Do your parents and extended family have an interest in getting to know your friends?
16. Do you introduce your close friends to your family?

17. Are your friends invited to family functions like weddings and holidays?
18. How is friendship defined in your culture?
19. Who were your closest friends growing up and why?
20. Do you consider close family members as friends?
21. How does one deepen a friendship?
22. How are friendships different at different stages of life?
23. Are you comfortable and free to make friends who are different from you (background, ethnicity etc.)?
24. Who was your most different friend and why?
25. What was the most challenging friendship you have been part of and why?
26. How are friendships influenced by culture and gender?
27. Are friendships between people of the opposite gender common? Are they socially acceptable?
28. What are the cultural and societal expectations of deep friendships (like calling on for help during crisis)?
29. A common saying is that "a friend in need, is a friend indeed." Should a friend be obligated or expected to help a "friend in need"?
30. Is there a role for friendship in career advancement and if so, how does it work?

Food

1. What was the best meal you have ever had? Why was it so special?
2. What was the most significant meal in your childhood, and why did you find it so significant?
3. What is the purpose or function of food?
4. What does food symbolize?
5. What role did food play in your house growing up?
6. Who was involved in making food in your childhood home? Why was this the case?

7. When you grew up, how was throwing away food viewed, has it shifted over the years?
8. In what ways did your parents emphasize or de-emphasize eating nutritiously when you were a child?
9. What types of dishes and recipes are passed on through the generations and how important is it to continue to pass them on to future generations?
10. What are some food-related customs or traditions that are common for significant non-religious events in your community? (e.g. moving into a new house, buying a car, opening a new business)
11. Are there specific foods served during births, reaching a certain age, weddings and funerals? What are they?
12. Which foods are forbidden or taboo to eat?
13. Is there a connection between what you eat and your health?
14. How do people link food to health?
15. How do you create a healthy food culture for yourself and those who live with you?
16. What are some of the food traditions you grew up with that relate to the period of pregnancy and the months following the birth of the child?
17. Who makes the food in your house currently? Why is this the case?
18. What is the role of food in relationships? (Family, Friends, Work)
19. What is common practice when it comes to dealing with leftovers?
20. How does food play a role in showing generosity (if at all) and does it differ depending on who you are showing generosity to?
21. Does food play a role in building relationships at work, and what would be examples of common practices in the work context?

22. How often is it appropriate to eat out (at a restaurant), and why do you believe it to be so?
23. Who is typically invited to join you or your family for a special meal (friends, family, colleagues, etc.)?
24. What role does food play in family-gathering traditions?
25. What is the significance of food in your community? Why is it deemed so important or unimportant?
26. What are some examples of religious festivals in the calendar where food plays a role?
27. Is it important that you take care of your body by eating certain types of food from specific sources for any of the following reasons: ethical, spiritual, cognitive, religious, social, longevity, health, financial?
28. What are foods that are believed to have healing powers or effects? Why is that?
29. What are some benefits of trying food from other cultures?
30. With the trichotomy between eating for health, comfort, or fellowship, what do you see as the balanced intersection?
31. How are modern food habits different from traditional ones in your community?
32. Give an example of what a traditional meal would consist of in your community?
33. How is being overweight viewed and has this view shifted in the last two generations?

Gender Roles

1. In your culture, who is typically considered the head of the household, the father (male figure) or the mother (female figure)?
2. What types of societal expectations do men and women have placed on them in your culture? For example, are women expected to handle domestic duties such as cooking, cleaning, and child-rearing, while men are expected to work outside the home?

3. What are your thoughts on a man staying home to look after the children and manage household responsibilities while the woman works? Do you agree or disagree with this idea, and why?
4. Does your spouse work? If not, was this a choice, or are there other factors at play?
5. How do members of your family, including husbands and sons, contribute to domestic chores and responsibilities?
6. To what extent are women allowed to work outside the home in your culture?
7. According to your cultural norms, are there specific jobs or professions that are traditionally associated with men or women?
8. How much do gender differences play a role in matters of inheritance and ownership in your culture?
9. What are the significant phases or milestones in a woman's life according to your cultural traditions and beliefs?
10. Similarly, what are the important phases or milestones in a man's life?
11. In what ways and settings are men and women allowed to interact in society according to your cultural norms?
12. To what extent are platonic friendships between men and women socially acceptable in your culture?
13. What are the specific roles and responsibilities of grandmothers, mothers, aunts, and sisters in your society?
14. Conversely, what are the specific roles and responsibilities of grandfathers, fathers, uncles, and brothers in your society?
15. Is it common for men and women to eat together in your culture, and do they typically eat at the same time?
16. Are there places that are designated for either men or women exclusively? If so, how do these spaces differ from one another?

17. How do you make men and women feel equally included whenever you ask for volunteers to manage a project or delegate an important task?
18. To what extent do you believe that men and women should receive equal pay for equal work in the workplace?
19. Under what circumstances do you think it is acceptable for a woman to manage a team or supervise men in a professional setting?
20. What did adults around you assume about you because of your gender growing up?
21. In your family, who was responsible for performing routine tasks around the house, such as doing the dishes, cleaning, or fetching water, especially in a rural setting?
22. In what ways are boys and girls treated differently in your culture?
23. In what ways do you treat young children differently because of their gender?
24. Are there any associations between cleanliness or uncleanliness and gender in your culture?
25. Is there a preference for having a boy or a girl baby in your culture? If so, what are the reasons behind this preference?
26. In what ways do you think your parents mirrored the expected gender roles of their culture and in what ways did they act contrary to those expectations or norms?
27. What limits does your culture put on your gender that you think are beneficial for your welfare and well-being? Conversely, are there any restrictions put on you that are not beneficial?
28. How do you address situations where either gender assumes the role of a victim to avoid their responsibilities?
29. How do you address and rectify misconceptions that others may have about the treatment of different genders in your culture?
30. What are some gender-based taboos prevalent in your culture?

31. To what extent should respect for culture and values make way for the acceptance of differing sexual orientations?
32. What are the primary concerns or fears faced by women in your society?
33. What are the significant concerns or fears experienced by men in your society?
34. What are the topics that men are more likely to discuss exclusively with other men?
35. What are the subjects that women are more inclined to discuss solely with other women?

Generational Relationships

1. How does age dictate roles in the society where you grew up?
2. On whom does the responsibility of child rearing fall and why?
3. What age is the expected age for marriage and why?
4. What age is the expected age for a woman to have her first child? Why is that?
5. In what ways do very young children participate in family gatherings?
6. How are school-age children expected to behave at family gatherings?
7. What is the role of adolescents in the home?
8. In what ways are children expected to have relationships with their cousins and aunts and uncles?
9. Are you expected to live near or with your parents as you get older and begin working? Why or why not?
10. In your culture, do multiple generations live in the same house? How do you feel about that?
11. In what ways is your greeting to the elderly in your community different from how you would address younger members of society?

12. Do you stand when someone older than you enters a room? Why or why not?
13. When there is an intergenerational meal, is a particular person or persons designated to partake of the food first? Why is that?
14. What do intergenerational meals look like, can everyone eat together or are certain age groups separated? If groups sit at different tables or places, who goes where, and which age groups sit together?
15. Is it customary to offer your seat to someone if they are older than you? Why or why not?
16. What is the expected age for retirement? Why is that the age?
17. What does a retired person do with their time?
18. Describe how age relates to power or sway within society.
19. Describe how younger generations view those who are older?
20. How formal were your interactions expected to be around your grandparents?
21. How are the elderly treated in your culture? Are they cared for by their families, or placed in an old age home?
22. Describe who offered wise counsel and gave support in your family, and how they did this.
23. How did your parents and grandparents relate to each other?
24. Was there a lot of interaction or engagement between multiple generations in your family or community and how do you think this shaped your worldview?
25. Do you value living close to your parents and siblings? Why or why not?
26. How do grandparents, parents, and children display affection toward one another in your culture?
27. What does generational respect look like in a work environment?

28. How is leadership within your community transferred between generations?
29. How have you seen your role within your family and work life change as you have grown older?

Generosity and Doing Good

1. How are charity and generosity expected in society?
2. How is generosity typically practiced? Anonymously? Publicly?
3. Can generosity be measured? If so, how?
4. What are some actions that would be considered especially generous?
5. If you receive something in return for doing good, does it count?
6. What is generosity in your culture?
7. Is generosity one of the values typically associated with your culture?
8. Who do you admire as a generous and benevolent person?
    a. What are their characteristics that make them this way?
    b. How do you think they became like this?
9. Is hospitality considered part of generosity? How is it practiced?
10. How is generosity instilled in children, if at all?
11. How would you respond if someone was "too" generous to you? What would be considered the appropriate response?
12. Can you be too generous?
13. What is considered the limit of generosity?
14. Is caring for and giving to the poor required in your daily life?
15. Is there a "bad" kind of generosity?
16. Who are the people you typically give to in your life and what form does this giving usually take?

17. Do gifts come with strings attached?
18. When you give a gift to someone do you expect anything from them in return?
19. Is it okay to expect others to be generous if you are generous?
20. Is it acceptable to be generous to people who are poorer or richer than you?
21. Which types of generosity are considered easier or harder?
22. How easy or difficult is it for you to be on the receiving end of generosity and good deeds?
23. What are typical ways people respond when they receive something beyond their expectations?
24. Under what circumstances can generosity be done publicly and when is it expected to be done privately?
25. When is talking about your generosity considered inappropriate? Or when does talking about generosity become linked with pride or arrogance?
26. Would pressure from others affect generosity?
27. Is your community more focused on doing "what's right" as perceived by the group or what's right according to some spiritual norms or laws?
28. What does it mean to be "good" in your culture? Which structure determines what is good? (Religion, government, families, etc.)
29. How is generosity practiced? Is it shown in charity (giving to organizations that do good work, e.g., among the poor and sick) or in hospitality?
30. Is generosity required in your religious practice?
31. What type of benevolence is most common and why? Hospitality toward people with less means, giving alms directly to a poor person, giving to a charity (an organization that does good to the poor, society), or giving to a religious organization?
32. Is volunteering common and how is that encouraged?

33. When is generosity expected to be reciprocated? Is it linked to debit and credit in relationships?
34. Are there types of good deeds practiced in society that don't improve the community in the long run?

Gestures and Nonverbal Communication

1. How significant is nonverbal communication within your culture?
2. Which specific gesture denotes approval in your culture?
3. In your cultural context, what connotations does pointing at someone carry?
4. Can you provide examples of non-verbal communication facilitated by objects or food within your cultural practices?
5. What unique gestures from your culture might be misunderstood elsewhere in the world?
6. How are whistles or brief tunes utilized in your culture, and what messages do they convey?
7. What are the customary ways to acknowledge someone from a distance without verbal communication in your culture?
8. How do traditional greetings differ based on gender in your culture?
9. Are there distinct non-verbal cues or gestures that convey particular meanings during both initial greetings and farewells?
10. How do individuals typically signal for someone to approach or draw nearer non-verbally within your cultural context?
11. What gestures are considered obscene or taboo within your cultural norms?
12. How is the act of touching someone of the opposite gender on the shoulder perceived in your cultural context?

13. What are common mistakes in non-verbal communication that individuals from outside your country might inadvertently make?
14. What are some gestures that convey messages without the need for words?
15. What gestures set individuals apart from the groups they are surrounded by?
16. From your culture, which gestures do you appreciate the most and which ones do you dislike?
17. Can you identify specific gestures that typically indicate people's emotions or feelings?
18. Are there gestures exclusive to interactions with children or adults, and what repercussions might occur if these gestures are confused or mixed up?
19. How does the choice of meeting location, the arrangement of the venue, and seating preferences serve as forms of non-verbal communication?
20. What specific non-verbal cues are utilized in negotiations to enhance the likelihood of success?
21. What are examples of appropriate non-verbal communication methods, such as the use of emojis in written forms of communication like text messages and emails?
22. Could you explain how non-verbal cues facilitate the management of turn-taking during conversations?
23. When communicating, who is responsible for making sure the message is understood, the sender or receiver?
24. How can one ensure they have interpreted a message in the manner intended by the communicator?
25. Can you provide examples of gestures and non-verbal communication that involve the entire body, such as posture, exiting or entering a room, and standing?
26. How important are the eyes in communication?
27. When verbal and non-verbal cues conflict, how do you address the discrepancy?

28. How often do you notice nonverbal clues that convey underlying emotions?
29. How accurate are you at interpreting nonverbal clues when you notice them?
30. Is silence considered a form of non-verbal communication, and how is it employed? Who is typically authorized to employ silence in communication scenarios?

Humans and Nature

1. Do you spend time in nature? If so, what activities do you typically engage in?
2. What role did nature play in your upbringing?
3. In your culture, what is the primary purpose of a nature park? Is it primarily for facilitating recreation, providing refuge for plants and animals, or protecting ancient sacred grounds?
4. Was environmental stewardship a prominent theme in the culture in which you were raised?
5. How has your relationship with the natural world evolved from childhood to the present?
6. Can you recall a specific instance when your perspective on your relationship with nature shifted? If so, what prompted this change and how did it occur?
7. How does your connection to the land contribute to your sense of home?
8. Is it possible for someone to have a sense of rootedness without a direct connection to the land?
9. How do you believe the connection between nature and culture should be taught to the younger generation?
10. Do you believe the world is beyond repair, or do you hold to the belief that all things can be made new?
11. Is a restored creation part of your worldview? If so, how do you contribute to the new creation?
12. What is your perception of the human condition?

13. How are nature and spirituality connected in your religious practice?
14. In your society, is there integration between your relationship with nature and your belief system?
15. Can you provide examples of what this integration looks like in practical terms?
16. Which holds greater importance to you: human life or all life (nature)? Why or why not?
17. Should humans act as stewards of nature (i.e. population control through hunting, game reserves, etc.) or should we seek to allow nature to flourish with as little influence as possible? Why or why not?
18. What are some effective practices from various cultures that you would adopt to promote protection and care of the land?
19. How has the view of nature you were raised with influenced your dietary habits?

Kids and Upbringing

1. What did your family value most growing up?
2. What was the most important thing your parents taught you growing up?
3. In which way is it significant to be the oldest or youngest born in the family?
4. What is interaction typically like between siblings?
5. What are common rites of passage for children in your community?
6. What are the stories that children are told? Rhymes? Myths/legends? Historical/cultural tales? Family lore?
7. To what extent is it necessary to have grandparents involved in children's lives in your community?
8. How are girls and boys perceived differently as they grow up?

9. What kinds of chores or responsibilities do children learn/have in the home and at what age do they start doing those things?
10. At what age should children start their formal education and why?
11. What age did you start your formal education? And why?
12. Why is culture important for kids to understand?
13. Is spanking children appropriate? When is it unacceptable/forbidden or appropriately viewed and used?
14. Why should children be disciplined? (Disrespect, disobedience, or defiance, etc.)
15. What types of discipline were used in your community to discipline children?
16. How have the types of discipline used in your community changed in recent years?
17. Are both girls and boys taught how to cook and clean? What is the reason for this?
18. Who is generally the primary caretaker/caregiver of the children in your family and community?
19. Growing up, were children shamed if they did something wrong?
20. Is it ok for the youngest girl in the family to marry first? Why or why not?
21. What roles do extended family members play in the upbringing of your child?
22. How important is it to have a strong connection with your in-laws for the sake of your children?
23. Who is the authority at home? The mother, father, both, or someone else?
24. At which age should kids first have sexual education? Why?
25. Is it common in your culture to have parents from two different cultural backgrounds?
26. With your role in the family, how do you model the important values and behaviors that you would like your kids to emulate and develop?

27. How did the way that you were raised communicate the spoken and unspoken values of your immediate family/family of origin?
28. If you are living in a different city or country than you were raised, how does raising children in a different culture enrich their upbringing?
29. Where have your kids grown up?
30. Which country do they feel is their home?
31. Which country is their favorite?
32. What are ways that children play in your culture—games? sports? toys?
33. Are there songs that children learn to sing?
34. How many children do families in your culture typically have? What is the gap between different siblings?
35. How are children seen in society and in families?
36. What was the most important thing your parents taught you growing up?
37. How have you seen your children influence positive change as a result of their exposure to a variety of cultures?
38. What are some practical tips that you can offer to those raising their children abroad?
39. Where does the rest of your family live?
    a. How often do you get to visit them?
    b. Do they get to visit you?

Leadership and Followership

1. What qualities make someone a leader?
2. What attributes make a leader worth following, and which do you admire most in good leaders?
3. What leadership style do you prefer?
4. Who is a leader you aspire to be like and why?
5. Who was the most inspiring leader you have met, and what made them inspiring?
6. Do you see yourself as a leader? Why or why not?

7. What factors influence the relationship between leaders and followers?

8. What are some lessons that you have learned recently from a leader–follower relationship that you are in?

9. What are the expectations of subordinates, and what are the boundaries regarding leaders asking for favors from them?

10. How appropriate is it for employers to make requests outside of regular office hours, and how do employees typically handle such requests?

11. Can employers request non–work-related tasks from employees, and is it considered appropriate?

12. How should employees handle their leaders continuously assigning them tasks that seem unimportant to the organization's success?

13. When is it appropriate for employees to ask clarifying questions or discuss potential issues like lack of expertise, resources, or time when given tasks by a leader?

14. Are you comfortable with disagreeing with your employer? Under what circumstances is this acceptable?

15. What impact would disagreeing with your employer (or employee) have on the relationship you have with them?

16. What is an effective approach for a leader to solicit opinions from their direct reports?

17. Is the leader primarily there to assist the team, or is the team's purpose to aid the leader? What's your perspective on this?

18. How do you become a leader in your community?

19. Who are the primary role models in your community?

20. Is being a leader a privilege for a few select people or can anyone become leader? Why or why not?

21. Are leaders always right in your culture? Why or why not?

22. To what extent would you disagree with a community leader? Why or why not?

23. In what contexts are you a leader and in which ones are you a follower? How easy is it for you to switch back and forth between those contexts?
24. How would you recommend someone whose leadership has been rooted in their position go about developing consensus-based leadership?
25. How does leadership differ in various contexts, such as family, work, or community?
26. What qualities do effective leaders in your community possess?
27. How do leaders in your community handle conflicts or disagreements?
28. Are leaders in your community typically appointed or elected? How does this process work?
29. What role does tradition play in selecting leaders in your community?
30. How do leaders in your community stay connected with the needs and concerns of the people they lead?
31. In what ways can leadership be both empowering and limiting in your community?
32. What strategies can aspiring leaders employ to gain support and trust from their community members?
33. What qualities define a good or bad leader in your community?
34. Which leadership roles are typically trustworthy and which are viewed with suspicion, and why?
35. Would you continue working for a bad leader if your financial situation allowed it? How would your decision differ if your income depended on the job?
36. What distinguishes good followers from bad ones, and how do their behaviors impact leadership?
37. Is it possible for a bad leader to be removed from their position, and if so, how would that typically be done?

38. What character traits or behaviors would make for a good leader but be bad for a follower and vice versa?

Money, Stuff, and Wealth

1. What is the purpose of money?
2. You may have heard it said that "less is more." What does this statement mean to you?
3. How is money perceived in your cultural context?
4. What are things that money can and cannot acquire?
5. In your culture, does anything hold greater value than monetary wealth?
6. Do you perceive a correlation between success and wealth? Why or why not?
7. What are some symbols of wealth and status in cultures worldwide?
8. Which possessions, such as watches, handbags, clothes, shoes, homes, or cars represent wealth in your culture?
9. How does money play a role in shaping parts of your culture?
10. Is wealth synonymous with honor in your culture? If yes, what contributes to this perception? If not, what motivates individuals to pursue wealth despite this?
11. Do you find that money equates to power in your culture? Why or why not?
12. How is wealth passed down from generation to generation in your culture?
13. Are you expected to share your wealth with extended family? How do individuals navigate these expectations?
14. Do family members frequently request financial assistance from you?
15. How does culture influence the act of saving money for the future? What are some methods of saving that are specific to your culture?

16. To what extent are wealthy individuals expected to be generous in your culture?
17. What is the impact of donating money in your culture, and how is it perceived?
18. How might someone do "good" with money in your culture? What is considered doing "bad" with money?
19. How does your culture perceive individuals who fall into poverty? Is poverty linked to shame or piety?
20. In your culture, who is expected to help those that are living in poverty? Why is this the case?
21. Where do individuals in need of funds for business ventures typically seek loans in your culture? How does the system of interest and repayment operate?
22. Is the practice of paying interest accepted in your culture?
23. How do investors in your culture make profit on their investments?
24. Do you think that a person's happiness is determined by their wealth? Why or why not?
25. In your culture, is having a substantial amount of money perceived positively or negatively?
26. Is it preferable to display wealth publicly or is it better to keep it private? Why or why not?
27. Which holds greater significance: money or happiness?
28. Do you think wealth management is a common practice for many people?
29. Is the pursuit of wealth a priority for you and your family?
30. Why is it that the rich become wealthier while the poor become poorer? What steps can be taken to maintain a balance?
31. It has been said that the problem with affluent countries is not their wealth but their perception of poverty. To what extent do you agree, and why?

Music, Film, Art & Expression

1. Does art matter? Why or why not?
2. How do you define art, and do you believe it is constrained by any factors?
3. What do you think is the importance of art in society and how should it be expressed?
4. Could you share your favorite movie with me, and what makes it personally significant to you?
5. When was the last time you encountered a piece of art that deeply moved you, and what about it evoked such emotions?
6. Do you think modern music is losing the cultural values it once had? If so, why do you believe this is happening?
7. Is there a universally accepted method of artistic expression, and are there forms of expression that are frowned upon?
8. In your community, how are individuals encouraged to express themselves through art in all its forms?
9. Are there street musicians in your area, and how are they perceived by the community? Do people typically stop to listen or offer financial support, and why do you think they are regarded in that manner?
10. When it comes to music, films, and art, do you believe there should be censorship, or should there be complete freedom of expression? What are your reasons for holding this viewpoint?
11. How do you personally express yourself?
12. How do music, film, and art bring different cultures together?
13. What role does music play in shaping cultural identity?
14. How does the music in your community reflect your culture? In what ways is it similar or different from the music of other cultures you've encountered?

15. What difference would it make to the world if more people supported the arts?
16. Are there particular genres or styles of music from other cultures that you feel a connection to?
17. Should art classes such as drawing, painting, or sculpting be included in K-12 school curricula? What are your reasons for supporting or opposing their inclusion?
18. Are the arts accessible to everyone, or are they typically reserved for the talented few?
19. What music styles are prominent in your community?
20. How do artists typically generate income? Is it through patronage, sponsorship deals, ticket sales, or sales of books/records?
21. In your culture, would pursuing a career as an artist bring honor or shame to your family? What are the reasons behind this perception?
22. In your society, how does the income of successful artists (such as writers, musicians, and actors) compare to that of individuals in other professions (like doctors, engineers, and politicians)? What factors contribute to this discrepancy?
23. How has music in your society evolved in the past few decades? In what ways has it remained unchanged?
24. Similarly, how has art in your society changed over the past few decades, and in what ways has it remained consistent?
25. What are the preferred music styles among different generations in your culture, and are these styles indigenous to your culture?
26. What music styles are unique to your culture?
27. Are music classes included in the K-12 school curriculum in your culture? If so, why do you believe children are typically taught to play instruments or sing?
28. How do music and religion intersect in your culture, if at all?

29. In what ways can music, film, and art be incorporated into worship practices?

Relaxation and Free time

1. How often does your family vacation together?
2. Do you consider "sitting" to be lazy and a waste of free time?
3. Are rest and recreation a priority for your family and community?
4. What are the usual relaxation activities of people across ages in your community?
5. What would be your perfect relaxation activity if time and money were unlimited?
6. Does your community create opportunities for members to spend their free time together through events and community activities?
7. How do you define "relaxation"?
8. Is the idea of relaxation different in different cultures?
9. What does "rest" look like for you?
10. How does rest differ from relaxation?
11. Do you value having free time to relax, or would you prefer more time to work?
12. Do you enjoy spending free time with others or by yourself?
13. If you typically relax with people, do you prefer to relax with family or friends?
14. How do you decide what to do with your free time? Do you make a plan or keep your options open?
15. In some company cultures, applying for your annual leave is seen as a lack of commitment to the company. Do you agree or disagree?
16. What activities are typical for a family at the end of a workday and during the weekend?

17. Is relaxation more about being active or being pampered/served?
18. How do you teach your kids the importance of relaxation and having free time?
19. Do you have consistent relaxation time set aside as a family?
20. In your culture and community, what do children consider relaxing and restful?
21. Do you think recreational activities can become future careers? If so, what are some examples?
22. Are certain recreational activities associated with societal standing, castes, ethnic groups, etc.?
23. Does watching a movie count as bonding time?
24. Do you think it is important to vacation by yourself and prioritize self-care?
25. How much sleep is too much?
26. When you have had a long and stressful week, what activities refresh and renew you?
27. If people spend money on free time and relaxation, what is considered "normal" and what is considered extravagant?
28. How much vacation time off would you prefer to have in a year? How much time is "too much"?
29. How do relaxation and free time differ across genders?
30. Are certain relaxation activities considered female-only activities? Are some considered male-only?

Religious Activities & Rituals

1. How often, if ever, do you pray or commune with a higher power? Are there specific times or rituals mandated by your religious tradition?
2. Do you view religious activities as superficial cultural practices, or do they hold real and significant meaning to you? What informs your perspective on this matter?

3. What are benefits you derive from participating in religious traditions and activities? How do they contribute to your overall well-being and sense of fulfillment?
4. To what extent does religion influence your life choices and decision-making?
5. Which religious tradition holds the most significance for you? How does this tradition contribute to your spiritual journey and sense of identity?
6. What is your perspective on integrating religious activities into societal institutions or public life?
7. Are there any religious practices which have disappeared in your lifetime? What may have led to their decline or total disappearance?
8. Which religious festivals or rituals are recognized as national holidays in your country? What led to this integration?
9. Do you see value in embracing a diversity of religions, or do you believe the world would be better off if everyone followed the same faith? What informs your viewpoint on this matter?
10. Is religion a personal choice or communal identity? Should children be taught their parents' religion or given freedom to explore their own spiritual path?
11. Regarding prayer practices in your religion, are prayers typically offered privately, within the family or group setting, or exclusively within places of worship? Is there a requirement for prayers to be led by ordained religious figures?
12. At what point does a child become an adult in the eyes of your community or culture? How is this transition typically marked or celebrated?
13. Is there a specific religious celebration or ritual associated with the transition to adulthood in your culture or faith tradition? If so, can you describe it?

14. How do you think your family and community would react if you decided to change your religious affiliation or identity? What challenges or support might you anticipate in such a scenario?
15. Are there any religious activities or practices mandatory for individuals to join a religious group or community? What about maintaining a good standing within the group?
16. If you could only pass on one religious practice to your children, which would you choose and why? What significance does this practice hold for you personally, and why do you believe it is important to impart it to the next generation?
17. How do you believe individuals should demonstrate respect for the religious activities and practices of others?
18. Is it acceptable for individuals outside of your religious community to participate in your religious activities and rituals? What factors influence this decision, and what are your thoughts on inclusivity in religious practices?
19. In your workplace, do people celebrate inter-cultural holidays and religious observances together, or do they tend to keep such celebrations within their respective cultural or religious groups?
20. From your perspective, how challenging is it for individuals who do not belong to mainstream religious groups to achieve success and integration in society? What barriers or opportunities might they encounter along their journey?
21. How do religious rituals shape cultural norms, values, and community interactions?
22. Reflecting on your upbringing, were there any religious traditions or activities that your family practiced, and how did they influence your understanding of faith and spirituality? What significance did these traditions hold for you personally?

23. How are atheists perceived and treated in your culture? Are there any common stereotypes or misconceptions associated with atheism?
24. Is religious practice considered a private matter in your culture? If so, what are some examples of acceptable private worship practices? How do individuals navigate the balance between personal faith and public expression of religious beliefs?
25. Do you have friends who belong to different religious groups? If so, what factors influence your friendships across religious lines? If not, what are some reasons for this?
26. To what extent is it socially acceptable to form friendships with individuals from different religious backgrounds? Are there any societal norms or expectations regarding interfaith friendships?
27. How does your society view romantic relationships between people of different religions? Are there any challenges or barriers faced by couples with differing religious beliefs?
28. What role did religious activities play in your family growing up? Were they central or more peripheral?
29. Upon leaving your family environment, did you continue to engage in religious activities? What factors influenced your decision to maintain or discontinue these practices?
30. What motivates you to participate in religious activities? Do you view them as a duty, obligation, necessity, source of enjoyment, or as a means of fostering community connections?

Religious Leaders

1. How are religious leaders regarded in your community?
2. In what ways do religious leaders influence and shape your community?
3. To what extent do religious leaders influence societal issues and political matters?
4. What qualities differentiate religious leaders from leaders in business or politics?
5. In your opinion, what should be the extent of the connection between religion and politics, and why?
6. How significant is faith and belief in God or higher spiritual powers in society and leadership?
7. How do religious leaders specifically make your community either better or worse?
8. How are religious leaders perceived in comparison to other leaders in your culture?
9. Are religious leaders generally respected, or are they viewed with skepticism and carefully managed?
10. What are the primary reasons why individuals may hold negative opinions of religious leaders?
11. Conversely, what are the main reasons why people tend to view religious leaders positively?
12. In terms of overall trust in leaders within your community, how do religious leaders compare to other types of leaders?
13. What sort of power do religious leaders hold over their followers?
14. What is the role of religious leaders in people's day to day lives?
15. What are the significant life events or milestones in which religious leaders play a crucial role in your community?
16. To what extent is your religious leader important to you, or how much authority do they have in your life?

17. In your community, who holds authority on spiritual matters, and how did they gain that authority?
18. To what extent do you trust your religious leader for guidance and advice?
19. Do you believe all leaders should possess spiritual awareness or adhere to a specific religious doctrine?
20. In your religion, what are the procedures or criteria for excommunication or severing ties with individuals?
21. Can you share an experience where you have either encountered pain or found healing through the actions of a religious leader?
22. To what extent is it acceptable for religious leaders to publicly shame people?
23. What are the consequences for those who question religious leaders in your community?
24. Is it necessary to seek approval from a religious leader for significant life decisions?
25. Do you see religious leaders' role as enforcing traditional rules or interpreting them in modern life?
26. How do you cope with the adverse effects that certain religious leaders may have on your well-being or beliefs?

Rituals and Rites of Passage

1. At what age does a child become an adult?
2. Is there a ceremony or celebration? Who is meant to attend? What is preparation like?
3. Did you have a coming-of-age ceremony?
4. Is this a practice you will maintain for your own family?
5. How do young people demonstrate they are "becoming adults"?
6. At what age are you considered a respectable member of the community?
7. Do teenagers have to complete a rite of passage to be considered adults?

8. Are there certain rituals and rites of passage connected to being part of a club or society (sports, scouts, orchestra, etc.)?

9. How does the family or community prepare boys for marriage?

10. How does the family or community prepare girls for marriage?

11. How is marriage perceived in your culture to change an adult's life?

12. Is there anything that your grandparents expected their grandchildren to do as a rite of passage? Did your parents go along with this desire out of respect, even if they did not support it?

13. Do you expect your children to carry on your family heritage through practicing the same rituals and rites of passage that you did with them? How will it affect your relationship should they choose not to?

14. Is there a particular age or experience that is considered a "milestone" in your adult life?

15. Do you think your culture's rites of passage impacted who you are today?

16. How would you be different had you not performed your family's cultural or religious rituals?

17. What was the most significant moment for you on your journey to adulthood?

18. When did you first become aware that there were certain rituals or rites of passage that were expected of you or of others in your culture?

19. What are the origins of your familial or cultural rites of passage?

20. Why are your culture's rituals and rites of passage important and what purpose do they serve?

21. Are there old rituals that your ancestors used to practice which you know have been lost?

22. What rituals and rites of passage are religious in your family or community? Which are cultural?
23. Are there any special rituals or practices with new-born infants?
24. What birthdays are especially significant in a child's life? Why?
25. Do you celebrate other passings of time besides birthdays?
26. When is someone considered an elder in your community?
27. Are there any rituals or practices to remember and honor people who have died?
28. Are there any rituals associated with the process of grieving in your culture?
29. Is death considered a rite of passage in your culture?
30. What are rituals and practices associated with the body after death?
31. Is there a specific place in which rituals surrounding the death of a loved one are performed?

Sacrifice

1. What does the word "sacrifice" mean to you?
2. What makes something a sacrifice?
3. Has anyone ever made a sacrifice for you? If so, why do you think they did it?
4. Have you ever sacrificed anything for someone else? Why did you do it?
5. What is the most significant example of sacrifice you have witnessed? Why was it significant to you?
6. How do you determine when a sacrifice is necessary?
7. How do you choose when to make a sacrifice?
8. Can someone sacrifice too much, or inappropriately? What is an example of where you have seen this?
9. Why are people who have made great sacrifices in history revered?

10. To what extent is it considered selfish to prioritize one's own needs over those of friends and family?
11. If someone makes a sacrifice for you, do you believe you are obligated to return the favor?
12. Are there differences in how different generations see sacrifice? How has this perception shifted over the last three generations?
13. What impact does sacrifice have on the recipient, and what do you believe is the appropriate response to it?
14. Do you think there are different societal expectations regarding sacrifice based on gender? If so, what are they?
15. Under what circumstances do you believe it's morally right to sacrifice for others?
16. Do you believe there's a limit to how far one should go when sacrificing for someone else?
17. Is there a limit to how much you would sacrifice for your family?
18. Do you consider it a sacrifice if fulfilling a duty or obligation?
19. Do you think true altruism is possible, and if so, how do you achieve it?
20. Should individuals relinquish their rights for the betterment of their community
21. Is there ever a situation where someone should be compelled or obligated to sacrifice their rights?
22. How would you distinguish between sacrifice and selfishness?
23. When do you think it's appropriate to sacrifice for others without expecting anything in return?
24. Have you ever felt pressured to sacrifice something for your community? What decision did you ultimately make, and why?
25. What are the implications of presuming someone's motives behind their act of sacrifice?

26. What does sacrifice in marriage entail, and how does it manifest in real-life scenarios?
27. Do you feel a sense of sacrificial obligation in your life? If so, in what aspects and to whom?
28. Reflecting on your priorities, what is the most significant aspect of your life, and what would you be willing to sacrifice for it?
29. Is sacrifice inherently beautiful? Why or why not, and what are the factors that influence its beauty?
30. In your opinion, what takes precedence: sacrificing personal desires for the sake of family, or sacrificing family ideals for personal desires? Explain your reasoning.
31. What obligations, if any, do children have toward their parents as a result of their parents' sacrifices? How can these obligations be expressed?
32. To what extent do cultural norms and personal values influence one's duty to sacrifice, and how does this duty vary in different contexts?
33. Can you recall instances in which you chose not to sacrifice something? What factors influenced your decision-making process?
34. How have stories of sacrifice, whether from religious texts, history, or personal experiences, impacted your understanding of sacrifice and its significance?
35. What is the most important thing in your life and what would you give up for it?
36. Do you consider sacrifice a beautiful thing? Why or why not?
37. What is more important—to sacrifice your own desires for the sake of your family? Or to sacrifice your family's ideals for the sake of your own desires? Why or why not?
38. What should you sacrifice for your parents? Do you owe them anything because of their sacrifice for you?
39. How far does your duty to sacrifice extend? And is there a right order for who it belongs to first?

40. Have you ever deliberately chosen not to sacrifice something? What led you to that decision?
41. Can you recall stories that you grew up with that exemplify sacrifice?
42. If you are religious, how does sacrifice play a role in what you believe?
43. How does religion influence the perception of sacrifice within your community?
44. In what contexts is sacrifice considered an expectation within your religious tradition, and what are the underlying reasons for this expectation?
45. Who holds the authority to determine whether a sacrifice is appropriate within your religious framework, and what factors contribute to this determination?

Social Values

1. Do you think social values are mostly the same across all cultures? Why or why not?
2. What are social values that are important and relevant in today's world?
3. Are social values the same for everyone in your community and culture?
4. What are some examples of violating social values?
5. What is a recent example you've experienced of the breakdown of social values in your society and culture?
6. What are ways you have seen initiatives (small or big) rebuild healthy social values?
7. Are certain social values prioritized for females as they become young women? What are these social values?
8. Are certain social values prioritized for males as they become young men? What are these social values?
9. Is hospitality an expectation in your home? Why or why not?

10. What is a social value demonstrated in your family that you appreciated as you grew up?
11. How were you taught to be obedient or "good" as a child? Was counsel from parents or elders an important part of discipline? Was corporal punishment an acceptable form of discipline?
12. How do your daily life choices reflect the values imparted to you by your parents? Have you adopted a different set of values as an adult?
13. What do you believe is the most important value for a person or a family to pursue for a successful life?
14. How does society treat a member who is a good person but behaves differently from what is expected in society?
15. What behaviors show whether someone is a good or bad person?
16. What characteristics does your community value most in a person?
17. What characteristics does your community value most in a company or business?
18. What characteristics does your community value most from community and government leaders?
19. What societal values were important to your friends growing up?
20. What societal values are valued most by your friends currently?
21. How do you decide who should be welcomed into your circle of friends?
22. Would you be friends with a person if their values were significantly different from yours?
23. What societal values, when followed, give a person status?
24. If you are living outside your home culture, what social values are shared between your culture and your host culture?
25. What are the main social values in your culture?
26. Which ones do you value the most?

27. How do you teach and share social values with your children?
28. What are some of the ways someone can violate social values? How does this affect the community?
29. How does the government instill and enforce the values that are important to the government?
30. What is the role of education in instilling social values?
31. Are there groups/tribes/subcultures in society that focus on different social values?

The Spiritual World and Belief in the Supernatural

1. What is the importance of the supernatural in your culture or society?
2. How important is it to "pray" or request help from an object of worship before you start a new project?
3. What are some examples of good or bad omens (*a happening believed to be a sign or warning of some future event*) in your society?
4. What is the role of (deceased) ancestors in your society? Do they need to be appeased and kept happy? Do they have the ability to influence the living by bringing blessings or curses?
5. What animals are sacred in society? What animals have supernatural powers (either live animals or animal products)?
6. What are the causes of sickness and accidents? Are they believed to be caused by natural causes or by supernatural causes (or both)? Give examples.
7. Which supernatural practices are 'common' in society but actually frowned upon or not talked about in general society?

8. Give some examples where certain actions or rituals are integrated in significant social events (e.g. birth, marriage, adulthood, opening a business, buying a car)?

9. Are certain spiritual practices connected to special individuals or groups in society?

10. If someone has special privileges or powers related to the supernatural, how are they passed on to other people (i.e., is it 'in the family')?

11. To what extent do animistic practices manifest themselves in orthodox religious practices?

12. How does the supernatural impact your daily life?

13. Is the spiritual world disconnected from daily life or seen as an integral part of it?

14. Is fate directed by each individual or is it already written?

15. In what ways can humans invoke the intercession of spirit beings in their lives?

16. What rituals or prayers are common at the start of a day, before eating, and before sleeping? Which ones do you practice?

17. How does one ask "god" or "the gods" for guidance/protection?

18. Do you believe in the supernatural?

19. Do your actions and beliefs in this life affect the afterlife?

20. Do you believe in miracles?

21. Do ghosts/spirits exist in this world?

22. Do you believe in a power greater than yourself?

23. Do you believe that there are things that cannot be seen but can be felt, such as a sense of who is going to call you before your phone rings?

24. Do you think we are humans having spiritual experiences, or spiritual beings having human experiences?

25. Is there anything beyond this world that we can observe?

26. Have you ever experienced anything you couldn't explain? What was it?

27. What agency do supernatural beings have in the lives of humans?
28. How important was the concept of "God (*A Higher Power or Being*)" in your household growing up?
29. What were you taught to be "afraid of" in the spiritual world?
30. Did your parents teach you about a variety of faiths as a child? Were you able to choose which one to believe or were you expected to believe the same as your family?
31. Were there measures your parents took to safeguard your home from the spiritual world growing up?

Sports & Exercise

1. Are sports an important part of the community in your culture?
2. How have sports impacted or shaped your community's culture?
3. What is the role of successful athletes or sports celebrities?
4. Are there certain people or groups in society who are expected to play sports? Are there certain groups who are expected to not play sports?
5. Are there societal or educational benefits for those who are good at sports?
6. What forms of exercise are encouraged in your culture?
7. Is there a place for exercise or sports in the work context? What are some examples?
8. How are nonphysical sports viewed (either mental games like chess or computer/online games)?
9. Does your country or city have climate or environmental conditions that influenced what sports were important and common?
10. How does your community view sport on the global stage?
11. How important is Sports in schools? Are sport and exercise prioritized in schools?

12. Are there certain sports that are encouraged to begin at a certain age? Is this true for girls and boys?
13. How important is it to introduce sports to children at a young age in your culture?
14. How is PE (Physical Education) viewed in education, specifically by gender? Is it viewed differently for girls and boys?
15. Were you physically active growing up?
16. Are rivalries between different teams common?
17. Are school teams cheered on by the entire community?
18. How do people view pursuing a career in sports?
19. Is exercise a priority for the elder members of your community?
20. Is there a difference in how the older generation and the younger generation view exercise and in which way has the level of engagement shifted?
21. How serious is the community about time around sports?
22. Is there a connection between sports and level of income, status, and ethnic background?
23. Is community identity tied to the success of a sports team?
24. Do you have a longstanding relationship with any sports teams? Why?
25. What is your favorite sport and your favorite team?
26. How do you prefer to exercise?
27. What are your favorite individual and group sports?
28. Do you play any sports? Why or why not?
29. Have you ever felt the need to learn a sport because it is part of a culture that interests you?
30. What level of emphasis did your family place on sports? How did that impact you?
31. Is it important that you take care of your body by exercising for any of the following reasons (spiritual, mental, religious, social, longevity, health, financial)?
32. What are considered to be the benefits of sports in your culture?

33. What sports or exercise activities are still practiced in your culture today that point back to old traditions or practices?
34. How much are women to be involved in sporting activities in your culture?
35. Are certain sports viewed differently for different genders?
36. Are women in your society encouraged to swim and are swimming costumes for women considered to be too revealing?
37. In which way does gender play a role in what is acceptable or not acceptable in sports?

Team

1. What is meant by "teaming," and how does it differ from traditional teamwork?
2. In your culture, is the concept of "teaming" highly regarded? What factors contribute to its value or lack thereof?
3. What is the primary purpose of assembling a team in your perspective?
4. What three essential qualities do you believe are necessary for a strong and successful team, and why are these qualities significant?
5. How do you instill the value of teamwork and being a team player in children?
6. In your opinion, how crucial is teamwork in achieving goals and fostering success in various aspects of life?
7. What specific role do you like playing on teams, and why?
8. Where did you first learn how to be a team-player?
9. Reflecting on your experiences, how easy or difficult is it for you to work on a team?
10. In your opinion, what characteristics and behaviors define a "good team leader"?
11. What qualities do you believe constitute an effective team player, and why are these qualities important?

12. Can you share an example of the best team you've been a part of, and what made it exceptional in your view?
13. When, if ever, is it appropriate to have side conversations during a team meeting, and why?
14. Can you describe a negative experience from the worst team you've been a part of, and what factors contributed to its dysfunctionality?
15. What is the role of social time in a team and how does it impact overall team performance?
16. What are reasonable expectations regarding "outside of work" social activities for team members?
17. If you were leading a team, what types of social activities would you organize to foster camaraderie and team cohesion?
18. How would you address underperformance by a team member within the group?
19. What factors contribute to creating a productive environment for teams, and conversely, what elements can make an environment unproductive for teamwork?
20. When you're a member of a team, do you typically address conflicts directly or indirectly? What factors influence your approach?
21. Why do you think teamwork can be challenging in certain environments or situations?
22. What do you find fulfilling or joyful about being part of a team?
23. What are some common challenges or difficulties experienced when working in a team?
24. In your experience, how is exceptional work recognized within a team?
25. In your opinion, how should a healthy team approach and manage conflicts?
26. In team meetings, how would disagreement typically be handled?

27. Do you believe that cultural diversity is important for team performance? Why or why not?
28. How does your team encourage and embrace ethnic diversity among its members?
29. What things are essential for building trust in a team?
30. How do you show loyalty to your team and how far would you go to express that loyalty?
31. How do you handle team members who exhibit toxic behavior?
32. Who is responsible for a team's success, and why do you hold this view?

Time

1. Is time considered abundant or valuable in your culture? Why is it regarded in this way?
2. Is it good to be in a hurry?
3. What are culturally acceptable reasons for being late?
4. Why do certain cultures place a strong emphasis on punctuality?
5. How is time typically allocated and utilized in your society?
6. Would arriving late to a meeting or event be considered impolite in your culture?
7. What are the durations of typical work meetings? Additionally, what proportion of these meetings is dedicated to building relationships, and what proportion is focused on accomplishing tasks?
8. In your culture, is it acceptable to close the doors to meetings once they have begun to prevent latecomers from entering?
9. If someone arrives late to an in-person meeting while you have arrived on time, how do you usually handle the situation?
10. How far in advance do you typically schedule meetings in your culture?

11. Are there specific types of meetings where flexibility or tardiness is acceptable, while punctuality is crucial for others?
12. Do you typically schedule time to meet with family or close friends, or do these meetings happen more spontaneously in your culture?
13. In your culture, how would someone be perceived if they abruptly ended a lengthy conversation in order to be on time for their next appointment?
14. Would you be offended if someone came an hour late to a dinner invitation?
15. If a close friend drops by unexpectedly but you have an important meeting to attend, how would you typically handle that situation?
16. In your culture, would it be acceptable to arrive late when meeting an important person, or is punctuality expected regardless of the circumstances?
17. Do you feel like you control your time or does time control you?
18. Is punctuality an important concept in your community?
19. How do you organize and manage your time?
20. In general, do you feel you have enough time?
21. What are typical sayings that relate to time in your culture?
22. What is your view of time and how do you show you value the time you have been given?
23. How do you wish you prioritized your time?
24. What do your weekends look like, are they booked full or free-flowing; what do you typically spend your weekend time on?
25. What is more important, showing people you care by being on time for them or showing them you care by being willing to be late for them?
26. Do you move into the future, or does the future come to you? Why do you believe that?

27. Is it possible to make up for lost time? How would you do that?
28. Is there a connection between how people handle time and their reliability and trustworthiness?
29. What is considered an appropriate way for older people to use their time?
30. Is your life worth living? What makes it worthwhile?

Trust

1. What does it mean to trust another person?
2. What behaviors can either build or destroy trust?
3. What qualities make a person trustworthy?
4. How can trust be developed at personal, interpersonal, and community levels?
5. Can you give examples of how products are more or less trusted based on where they were produced, or which company produced them?
6. Which leadership roles in society are generally perceived as trustworthy or untrustworthy, and have these perceptions changed over the past few generations?
7. What are some common tactics criminals use to exploit trust and deceive people out of money or possessions?
8. How can individuals show that they are trustworthy?
9. Can you recall a time when someone betrayed your trust? If so, how did it happen?
10. What does it take to restore trust after it has been broken?
11. Are there cultural rituals that help in restoring trust when it is broken?
12. Have you ever broken someone's trust? Describe what you did to regain it.
13. What did you have to do to restore the relationship when you broke someone's trust?
14. To what extent does one's outward appearance influence the level of trust they receive from others?

15. When someone is forgiven, does this automatically imply that they have also regained the person's trust? Why or why not?
16. To what extent do you value trust in relationships with people who are close to you?
17. To what extent does keeping your word equate to being trustworthy?
18. How do you build trust with your spouse or partner?
19. How many people do you genuinely trust in your life?
20. When it comes to legally binding decisions, would you take someone at their word or require a contract? Why?
21. How do you build trust in your culture?
22. Do you believe it is acceptable to break a promise? If not, why?
23. How much do ethnic or religious backgrounds influence trust or distrust between groups in society?
24. Were there specific nationalities or ethnicities you were taught to trust or distrust growing up, and what were the reasons given for those beliefs?
25. Are leaders in various societal roles expected to maintain consistency in their public and private lives in order to gain your trust?
26. What are the potential consequences of placing trust in someone?
27. Do you tend to trust authority figures or approach them with skepticism? Why do you feel that way?
28. How does your society treat people who are in authority (politicians, law enforcement. . .) once they have proven themself untrustworthy? Are they able to maintain their position?
29. Can you recall recent instances in your community where trust was broken or restored, indicating a trend of either growing or declining trust?

30. Do you or have you ever entrusted important decisions in your life, such as marriage, family, or career choices, to someone else?
31. In your community, can you think of recent stories of broken or restored trust that seem to indicate a growth or erosion of trust?

Work Relationships

1. What does friendship look like in an office environment? Are there specific behaviors or interactions that define workplace friendships?
2. To what extent do you believe it's important to invest in work relationships? Why?
3. During lunch or coffee breaks, do colleagues tend to eat together or alone? What factors influence this behavior?
4. Are your relationships at work strictly business-related, or do you interact with your colleagues in a personal capacity? Why do you prefer your relationships that way?
5. What characteristics define a good work relationship? Is it primarily about productivity, friendliness, strategic importance, collaboration potential, or a combination of these factors?
6. Do you enjoy attending work parties? Can you explain the reasons behind your preference?
7. If you're close with your colleagues, do you socialize with them outside of work? What types of activities do you typically engage in together?
8. To what extent do you share personal matters with your coworkers? Are you aware of details about your coworkers' families, hobbies, or other personal aspects of their lives?
9. What does it take for your work friendships to become personal friendships?

10. Do you consider your work friends to be as close as your "real friends" outside of work, or do you perceive a distinction between the two? Why or why not?

11. What are the most prevalent methods for securing employment through friendship connections in your experience or observation?

12. What are the potential benefits and drawbacks of giving friends and family preferential treatment during the recruitment process?

13. To what extent can employees be considered "untouchable" within an organization because of their friendship connections?

14. Is it acceptable to organize "fun" events such as celebrations and holiday parties in the workplace? What are the potential benefits or drawbacks of such activities?

15. How would you react if a coworker contacted your family without your consent to arrange a celebration or event for you?

16. If somebody is underperforming on a team, to what extent is this change how the matter addressed if a friendship has formed between the superior and the subordinate?

17. How are disagreements handled on your team once friendships have formed between team members?

18. If you need a favor from a coworker in a different department, are you able to ask for this favor directly, or do you have to ask his or her boss?

19. Are you more comfortable in a highly structured environment where it is clear who is the leader and who is the follower?

20. How are meetings expected to run in your culture? Who leads them, and who is only required to participate?

21. What would happen if you challenged your superior in front of other staff members?

22. In what circumstances is it appropriate to voice a concern or question to your superior and does this change if they are your friend?
23. How friendly and approachable should a leader be to their team?
24. How are the principles you use to lead at work different or similar to the ones you use in your family?
25. Is the customer always right or are there instances when they are not?
26. How do you relate to or connect with customers?
27. Where will you draw the line between giving a client an excellent experience and maintaining dignity and respect of your team?
28. Should loyalty be viewed as the highest priority in a relationship with a supplier, or should another value be prioritized? Why do you say so?
29. Are the personal relationships you build with clients and suppliers for the purpose of work, or are they real friends?
30. To what extent is it appropriate to give special favors or discounts to clients who are family members or friends?
31. Who decides what the expectations are in a relationship outside the office—your boss or you?
32. Is it acceptable to be friends with your boss?
33. Are romantic relationships with co-workers or bosses permissible and are there rules about how they should be conducted?
34. How would you respond if your boss invited you to watch a movie with them, or do something social outside of work hours?